D1743983

Patricia Hughes and her husband have been happily married for five years. After spending most of her life working and living in Brisbane, she is now a full-time writer enjoying the climate and life style of the Gold Coast in Queensland. Currently embarking on a sequel to the best-selling *Daughters of Nazareth*, she is looking to expand her writing into a range of crime fiction novels.

ENOUGH

Patricia Hughes

Spinifex Press Pty Ltd
504 Queensberry Street
North Melbourne, Vic. 3051
Australia

women@spinifexpresss.com.au
http://www.spinifexpress.com.au

First published 2004

Cover design by Deb Snibson
Typeset by Palmer Higgs Pty Ltd
Printed and bound by McPherson's Printing Group

National Library of Australia
Cataloguing-in-Publication data:
Hughes, Patricia, 1955– .
   Enough.

   ISBN 1 876756 40 3.

   1. Hughes, Patricia, 1955–. 2. Abused women – Victoria –
Biography. 3. Abused women – Victoria – Services for. I.
Title.

   362.8292092

In this book names have been changed to disguise identities.
Any resemblance to any individual of the name used, living or
dead, is both coincidental and unintentional.
The author and publishers have attempted without success to
trace the author of 'The Seven Steps' but this contribution is
acknowledged with gratitude.

Australia Council
for the Arts

This project has been assisted by the Commonwealth Government
through the Australia Council, its arts funding and advisory body.

For David
Once more, you are my anchor.

Acknowledgements

I would like to thank Councillor Toni Bowler for Redland Shire Council; both Sonia Lonne and Neil Wiseman, Counsellors for Interact Counselling Services; Thea Biesheuvel, the Chairperson of 'Survivors of Domestic Violence'; and Professor David Myers from the Central Queensland University. I am truly grateful for their endorsements and support during the publishing of my book. Their help and encouragement made the process and the results even more satisfying.

Foreword

The timing of the release of this powerful book couldn't be better. This deeply emotional account of one woman's devastating experience of violence at the hands of her male partner will serve as a reminder to all who read it of the culture of violence engulfing our world at the beginning of this twenty-first century. To our shame, future generations will look back on this period in history and identify it as one of the most violent periods ever—with the incidence and severity of war, terrorism, domestic violence and other forms of family violence increasing every day.

Of all the expressions of violence occurring throughout the world, men's violence against women and children in the home is the most constant and, arguably, the most heinous. Domestic terrorism. Women and children in huge numbers living with terrorism in their own homes, weighing up every word they say, always on edge, afraid to relax, doing their best to please their persecutors while all the time knowing that their best will never be good enough to prevent the next attack.

Those who work to provide safe places for, and

relieve the suffering of victims/survivors of domestic violence have puzzled for many years over the fact that societies everywhere seem willing to tolerate extreme levels of violence against women and children by their male partners and ex-partners. Why, they ask, are governments not outraged at the atrocities perpetrated against women and children in their homes to the point that they are motivated to put effective measures in place to stamp it out?

A look at the broader picture of male violence suggests that there is a definite link between violence in the home and violence expressed in acts of terrorism and war, and that domestic violence is allowed to continue because it suits the purposes of those in power around the world to condone and even encourage men's violence. Terrorist leaders, for example, would be unable to carry out their lethal work without followers who were familiar with violence and who were ready and willing to kill and be killed whenever the call came. Similarly, leaders of nations prepared to wage war against other nations for territory or oil or in the name of a 'war on terrorism' would be unable to achieve their lethal goals without an army of soldiers (mainly men) who had been encouraged all their lives to value competition and combat with the aim of winning. Dominate or be dominated. Kill or be killed.

This realisation that male-dominated governments are willing to tolerate and even condone men's violence against women and children as part of a larger agenda has women everywhere crying out: Enough!

As Patricia Hughes demonstrates so powerfully in the following pages, domestic violence is more than just a 'curtain raiser' for a bigger event. It is an event in itself and must be treated with all the seriousness accorded to any other life and death event. Every time a woman is assaulted, raped, degraded, mutilated or murdered by her partner or ex-partner, it is an event requiring the most urgent attention from government and community leaders. Every society has a responsibility to respond to domestic violence as effectively as possible, but what we see is that the response varies according to the basic philosophy of those in power at any given time. There are three possible approaches: conservative, liberal and radical.

The conservative approach is to ignore the existence of domestic violence based on the belief that the man is the head of the family and that it is his right to discipline the family in whatever way he sees fit. Embedded in this approach is the belief that a man would only resort to violence if he is provoked. An extreme version of the conservative approach is that employed by the Taliban in Afghanistan where a woman was to be seen and heard only through her husband or other male member of her family. If she complained or offered an opinion, she could and should be punished. In most Western countries, the conservative approach is less extreme but still serves to render women, and the violence perpetrated against them, invisible.

The liberal approach to domestic violence is the one favoured by the majority of governments and communities since the 1970s. Liberalism focuses on the situation at hand and deals, in a 'Band-aid' way, with what it perceives to be the needs of the individuals involved in what is often called 'a violent situation'. Provision is made for victims to be moved to a safe place and offered support and counselling. The perpetrator is advised to seek counselling aimed at delving into his childhood with a view to discovering clues as to why he behaves as he does or, if charges are laid, he can be required by the court to attend a perpetrator group or an anger management course. In addition, acting on the false assumption that violence is nothing more than a relationship problem, conflict resolution courses or relationship counselling are often recommended.

The radical approach, proposed by feminist researchers and workers in the field for many years, is quite different. Instead of naming a situation where a man abuses his partner as 'a violent situation' or 'a violent relationship', radicalism is careful to name it as it is: a violent man abusing his partner. The radical view is that justice is done only when the naming is accurate, and that a situation where a victim is placed in a position where she must take part of the blame for her own victimisation is not just. If both partners want to aim for reconciliation some time in the future, radicalism insists that the counselling they receive start from a position of honesty and justice.

The radical approach goes much deeper than simply working with individual women and men. It actually seeks to cut to the root of the problem of domestic violence and that means focusing on societal and group attitudes rather than on individual behaviour. Any government seriously wanting to rid its community of the scourge of domestic violence would employ a radical approach. They would begin by asking questions like: Why do men and boys use violence with such ease? Why do non-violent men and boys feel so much pressure to fall into line? Why do so many men appear to hate women? How early in life does the desire to degrade women and girls begin? How can government and community leaders change the present masculinist culture of violence into a culture of harmony and acceptance?

This book, carefully crafted and brilliantly presented by Patricia Hughes, advocates a strong radical approach to men's violence in the home. Analysing her own devastating experience, she is unequivocal in her view that there is no excuse for men's violence and no excuse should be sought. The only acceptable attitude to such violence is that it must stop and that perpetrators be held accountable for their actions. The positive message in the pages to follow is that, when victims receive the kind of support and encouragement they need and are enabled to make decisions in their own time, healing and a new start in life are very real possibilities.

Betty McLellan
Psychotherapist

Author's Note

How can love and commitment so easily turn to abuse and brutality? Why does this keep happening? Too many of us have asked these same questions after an episode of violence at the hands of a partner. Too many of us have known a woman who is unable to leave the man who beats her. We've cried with her, hugged her, taken her to hospital, made cups of tea for her; we've given her names and phone numbers of solicitors, psychiatrists and police. Yet, even though the beatings get worse each time, she still doesn't leave him. 'Why *doesn't* she leave?' people ask. 'How can anyone keep putting up with *that*?'

The ones who *do* manage to leave are the survivors. For most of us, this requires facing change, even danger. As a survivor of domestic violence, I know by taking certain steps a woman can take control of her own life and free herself. Life *can* be positive and worth living.

Domestic violence is complex. It is like a thief in the night, destroying and devastating its victims. It causes damage, both physical and psychological, leaving lasting scars. It can creep in slowly with verbal humiliation or it can be sudden and surprising as a bullet, horrifyingly physical. It betrays love, ends trust and destroys lives.

Fear, confusion, dependency and anger then surrounds the relationship and freedom seems impossible. Yet it *can* be stopped and freedom *can* be obtained. Many victims of domestic violence become free and remain that way. They obtain safety, end their abuse and heal. Some victims leave, only to return to their abusers many times before making the final decision to remain free. Some never get free at all.

Domestic violence is the single most common source of injury among women between the ages of fifteen and forty-four, more common than car accidents, muggings and rape by a stranger combined, and accounts for approximately twenty to twenty-five per cent of visits by women to emergency rooms.

There's no easy fix. No ready solution. History often carries with it the presumption that things change for the better, that somehow the passage of time will bring improvements. This doesn't help the women of today. With so much stacked up against those who don't leave abusive men, help of some sort is more important than ever. But no-one ever seems to be there to tell actually how to do it.

Hopefully, that's where I can help. I know the pitfalls and the signs and I also know how important it is to evaluate your life and especially your prospects.

There are seven identifiable steps which can be taken and these are included at the end of my story. They helped me through those dreadful times. These steps are not easy, but they can be accomplished. They forced me to face what I was doing with my life, to question myself and my relationship.

I hope these steps help other women too.

Patricia Hughes

Contents

Chapter One

The Look

When friends talk about the old days, some ask 'Do you remember just how bad it was?' and I say 'Hell, yes; it doesn't take much to bring it all back'. Sometimes all it takes to remind me is a sound or a smell. Sometimes it's the fiery glow of a cigarette tip; other times it's a spoken word or someone's mannerism that makes me remember those dreadful times.

When I think back to Kelly, it was the look that reminded me: the split lip, the bruise on her cheekbone, the averted glance looking everywhere except into my eyes. I remember the girl looked weary. Her shoulders were rounded as if the world weighed heavily on them and her blonde hair was pulled back into an untidy ponytail with no concern for style. Her eyes darted everywhere; like a scared child caught doing something wrong. Oh yes, I certainly remember *that* look.

Once in a while a piece of our history surfaces, some item we thought we'd dealt with and put behind us. Suddenly, it's there again at the top of the page, competing for attention despite the fact that we're completely unprepared for it.

The hardest thing for people to do is to admit they have a problem. Not just to say they have one but to say what it is, and then to admit it to themselves.

'My name is Joe Blow and I'm an alcoholic.' That sort of thing. And if it's done properly, everyone stands up and applauds—because admitting that we know about our problem is half the battle.

Well, it's my turn now.

My name is Patricia Hughes and I was once a victim of domestic violence.

Ten years ago, the main objective in my life was to put my past behind me and forge on to a better future. It was to be my time to find myself. My marriage separation was six months behind me and the world was my oyster.

Don't rush into anything, everyone told me. Have time by yourself, they all said. What is it that makes us think we're smarter than everyone else? That we know more than all of them combined? I know now I should have listened to them but hindsight is a wonderful thing. I have learnt now to accept the events I'm about to tell. Accept the dark hours and days and the solid recollection in between.

Somehow, I believed everything would be all right. And yet...

The 'and yets' of life are what slow us down. A wild rabbit casually grazes on clumps of grass by the side of a road and yet there's rustling among the leaves and ferns as if it's not alone. People seem happy and open and yet we have a feeling that they're only wearing masks and that deep down a lot of them feel lost. Most of the time, my life felt like a dream but not one I would wake up from gently.

I had allowed my life to be like a ferris-wheel, full of ups and downs, so at age thirty-five I had been determined to make a fresh start. Do something with my life, although I had no idea what that 'something' was.

Then, ten summers ago, my life changed overnight. I wasn't to know how much until later.

'I'd like a cheese and tomato sandwich, please,' the girl mumbled to her shoes.

At that time, with the horror in my past, I was trying desperately to maintain my coffee shop which was next to a railway line at Wynnum, a quiet bayside suburb inhabited mainly by elderly people who liked nothing better than to sit and watch the tide wash in and out of Moreton Bay. Unemployed teenagers spent most of their days in the amusement centre down the road from my shop, partly because lack of funds restricted them from doing much else but mainly because there was nothing to do in

Wynnum anyway. Even so, every Monday morning without fail, I would see the railway's commuter-parking lot across the road from my shop covered with beer cans flattened like pieces of roof tin by the dozens of cars which parked there.

By then, life had settled down a little for me.

Ten years. Three thousand six hundred and fifty days. Plenty of time for wounds to heal, you'd think. But even emotional wounds need to be dressed and attended to, as I constantly remind myself. Even when it was finally over, restless ghosts walked around in my head clanking their chains.

Over the years, these recollections have become fewer and fewer but still, occasionally, when my mind is idle, memory bubbles from those days slowly rise to the top before I have time to burst them. When the events from that time come to mind, it's like I clambered up from the depths, blinded by the darkness of my history, and teetered for a long time on the lip of a chasm, breathless, struggling to get a hold on my life.

'Would you like white or wholemeal?' I gently asked the girl on the other side of my counter.

She would have been considered attractive. She had large soft brown eyes, 'cow eyes' I called them, her figure was slim under her shapeless dress and the lines around her eyes were barely visible although a small frown was beginning to furrow her brow. I put her age at no more than twenty-five.

'White, please,' she said, and then touched her swollen lip self-consciously, averting her eyes again.

As I buttered the bread, I allowed my mind to wander backwards in time. I remembered the many occasions when my own face had been bruised and swollen. I remembered my own cut lips and the feeling that I was spinning out of control in a whirlpool with no idea how to get myself out. I remembered the coppery taste of blood in my mouth and the confusion I felt afterwards.

Remember? How could I ever forget?

Chapter 2

The Importance of
Frilly Pants

At five years old, growing up in The Valley in Brisbane, I had no doubts about how the world worked. In those days, I thought the worst thing that could happen to me was that I wouldn't be able to skip across the road to watch the TVs in the window of the electrical store, with my tomato sauce sandwich in my hand. I was oblivious to the pressures my parents were under in their daily struggle to survive in, what was then, a very poor part of town. I had no idea how much money there was after my father put his bets on racehorses or how much was left over after my mother came home drunk from going to the pub after work.

In 1960, it was fashionable for little girls like me to be dressed in frilly underpants with ruffles so that their skirts stuck straight out. Thank God my parents couldn't afford that luxury.

I can remember how I felt as I sat in the gutters, playing with my peg family, wearing a pair of scruffy over-sized pants bought from the local second-hand shop, while other little girls walked past me in their pretty pink dresses with their stiff underpants showing. I can still hear the scratchy sounds every time they moved and I can only imagine how the starched ruffles scratched the tops of their legs. Scored more deeply in my memory is the image of them bending over in public, flashing their frilly bottoms. For me, performing underpants were not an option.

In those days, before the real-estate developers saw Spring Hill's potential, the streets were strewn with litter, thrown there by the poor, the uneducated and the revellers, all of whom were my neighbours. But I remember being happier there than at any other place in the next fifteen years.

Life seemed carefree because none of my parents' struggles meant anything to me: until three days short of my seventh birthday, that is. That was the day I found myself on my way to Nazareth House, an orphanage and home for abandoned children in Brisbane. *Then* I knew.

Overnight, it seemed, my life changed and so did I. Over the next five years in the home, through many different foster homes, through the sexual and physical abuse in a number of them and through the confusion of abandonment, I changed.

Up to the age of seven, I was a happy, carefree little girl; a tomboy really. When I arrived at the orphanage, I became quiet and reserved. By the age of twelve, I was an unruly, angry, bitter adolescent on the outside, but screaming for help on the inside. At age fifteen, after I ran away from the home of my adoptive parents, I reverted back to being shy and introverted, a skittish creature scared of any human contact even though love was what I craved.

Maybe because the frilly underpants are such a powerful childhood memory, I started to think that femininity began in an outward way: girls dressed in girly dresses, played with dolls, brushed their hair and preened themselves while dreaming of knights in shining armour. The clear message to me was that girls should be elaborately fragile and doll-like.

So I changed yet again, this time into what I imagined was a demure young lady. Like a chameleon, I was trying to adapt by changing my appearance. But it doesn't matter how you disguise the outside, you can't change the feelings on the inside. That's the reality. The complexity for me was that while I may have been inappropriately hostile, the frilly pants had told me that I was supposed to be perfectly passive. Such is the power of memory. Now, I know that my ability to look at and feel good about myself lies embedded in my own early emotional experiences.

But life goes on and wounds *do* begin to heal. And so did mine. I married, had two beautiful boys but then, twelve years later, found myself going through a divorce. I realised that I had moved myself from one situation of subjugation to another. Though better than the orphanage and the foster homes, this way of life was not something I could accept permanently. I moved myself and my two boys to a house in the Redlands, a part of Brisbane that doesn't evoke any curiosity at all, where there was no mystery, no excitement; just a suburb like many others standing guard between Moreton Bay and the city. A sentry almost.

Within months of the separation, I realised I was doing my chameleon act again. Trying to change my personality, I laughed too hard at jokes when I really didn't see anything funny at all. Changing my appearance, I tried to show the world 'See? It's the new me', even though I had no idea who 'me' really was. I wanted to be outgoing and bubbly but had no idea where or how to start. When I looked in the mirror, I saw a pleasant not pretty face, fine blond hair that I wore to my shoulders and a thin body of average height. I felt depressingly ordinary and inadequate. After thirty-five years, it was a miserable tally of assets.

At the time, I didn't make friends easily. I still don't, to be honest. I withdrew from the few that I had and I left more behind at the separation, like part of the divorce settlement.

I remembered some of the girls at school with me. So happy and full of life—and good looking. All the attributes I lacked but longed for so much.

One of my few friends at school was Judy. I looked up to her. She was everything I wanted to be. I sometimes used to wonder why she let me walk around with her but it was nice to simply bask in the warmth of her popularity. I think I came out of my shell for a while thanks to Judy. The reason we weren't friends for longer than those three years was because I ran away from those last parents at fifteen. Life, I'd discovered, was full of disappointments. Happy times passed away, dreams never materialised.

In the early days of my marriage separation, I phoned the orphanage where I'd spent five years of my childhood. I was looking for my elusive family or, more to the point, a sister. I was told that there was none.

One thinks, at times like this, of the different courses that people cut through life. For some, it seems simple. They don't hesitate. They are beautiful and intelligent and life opens up to them as the Red Sea opened up to Moses.

Others have a constant struggle. They are shy. They stutter. They stumble. They never lose their self-consciousness. They talk when they should be silent or they are silent when they should speak up. When they hear laughter they assume it is directed at them. Though smart, they feel stupid. Though creative, they feel dull. Their passage through life resembles a person wading through mud. All these characteristics were mine. And were those of others I've known.

For instance, when I was in Grade 8, Margaret was the smartest girl in my school. She lived alone with her mother. Her father had disappeared when she was two. She had white hair, white skin and pink rabbity eyes and she blinked constantly behind the thick dark lenses of her glasses. She was overweight, a victim of treats—chocolates and lollies—that her mother gave to her, which was her way of apologising to her for the fact that Margaret was different from other girls. She was short and only grew to five foot tall. And she was shy. She was known as Pinky, a cruel name given to her by the other children.

On warm days, when most kids ran around in shorts and t-shirts, she was still bundled up and she couldn't participate in sports. I talked to her occasionally but she found it a torment and I soon gave up. People might say it isn't fair, but what has fairness to do with anything?

Some people appear to make it all the way through life without a mishap. They lead happy lives and leave behind happy children. Others go through life lonely and alone.

Ten years ago, I found myself lonely. Not alone because I still had my boys, but lonely, and this played a large part in the events that followed. It was a time when my life felt suspended, 'on hold'. We feel this way sometimes in our adolescence where there's a burning impatience for the next part of our lives to take shape and I'd felt like that every now and then in that year. I didn't know what it was that I wanted: I only knew it wasn't what I had. As much as I tried to rid myself of the feeling, it lingered persistently. I guess I wished for excitement.

And that's what I was thinking the Monday night before everything changed, before my nightmare caught up with me: the turning point in my life, such as it was.

I was poised exactly between the things of life I wanted to do and those I needed to do and I hoped for a moment that they were the same. And at thirty-five years of age, I thought I understood the nature of evil. I soon learned that I did not. I call this period in my life, 'Ordeal by Michael'.

I first met Michael when I worked at Pizza Hut. We

were both managers at different huts but, every few months, the powers-that-be held 'area conferences' so we could either gloat or commiserate with each other, depending on our store's performance.

This was to be my last such meeting. I'd resigned from Pizza Hut the previous week and my last working day was to be in another week's time. My husband and I had separated and I was determined not to be the sort of mother that I'd had when I was young. A mother who was always out, leaving me to fend for myself. Even if, at the time, I thought it was pretty good. (And what kid wouldn't? No rules. No regulations. No discipline.) But as an adult, with kids of my own, I knew that those things were necessary. And so was a mother who was a constant in her children's lives. So I resigned from Pizza Hut, to give my children everything *I* hadn't had when I was growing up.

It's not like Michael was strikingly handsome or that he stood out in the crowd, because he didn't. To tell the truth, I hadn't even noticed him. It was during the drinks at the end of the conference that another manager I vaguely knew came over to me.

'I have a friend who'd like to meet you.'

That was it. No build up. No talk about how this

friend thought I was so attractive. No flattery at all, just that he'd like to meet me.

He pointed Michael out and still I wasn't impressed. Michael was sitting in a booth by himself nursing a drink, an almost sullen look on his face.

'I don't think so, Miles.'

The party was in full swing by now and I hadn't even had a chance to get around to all the people I already knew. I was in a great mood and his friend's dark, surly James Dean looks did not really appeal to me.

'Yeah,' he said, swaying a little on his feet. 'I told him you'd think you were too good for him.'

'What?' I was flabbergasted. The statement was ridiculous. But then, hadn't others I worked with said that they'd thought I was a snob in the beginning? They'd had no idea that it was shyness, not snobbery, which made me keep to myself.

Faces swam around me, people I didn't know and some I'd *never* know. All of my life, because of those five years in the orphanage, I'd been closed up like a locked door, which hadn't helped my twelve-year marriage. Happiness and contentment seemed part of a world so far forbidden to me. It seemed logical for me to assume that eventually the odds would turn in my favour. Surely, it was *my* turn. After two drinks, I truly believed that.

You'd think I'd have known better.

'Make a liar of me and have a drink with him.' Miles hiccuped and staggered away leaving me standing by myself. I peered through the mass of people. Michael was still sitting there by himself. Eighteen months later, I would remember this night as the start of my downward slide into deeper pain.

Most of us are only aware of the superficial aspects of another's behaviour. We see the polite part, the public part and may not give a thought to what exists beneath. If the surface is conventional, we assume the rest to be the same. But, even so, why I walked over to his table, when I wasn't looking for any sort of a relationship, I'll never know. He didn't even fit the model of what I'd class as attractive. He had almost black hair, he was too thin for my liking and his nose had been badly broken at some time in his life. His eyes were too small and never looked at anyone else's. Recently, I read somewhere that eyes are the window to the soul and if I'd known that then, I would never have lived in hell for a year and a half.

The words 'if only' come to my mind as I write. If only I hadn't stayed for those drinks after the meeting at Pizza Hut. If only I'd stopped at *two* drinks and gone home to my sleeping children. If only I'd had one *extra* drink and been puking it up in the ladies. If only I'd never walked over to Michael at all.

Sometimes, even now, I dream about that moment. Of what would have happened if I hadn't decided to go to his table that night. And sometimes, in my dreams, I do actually walk out of the meeting and get into my car—then, if I'm lucky, I don't wake up screaming.

But, no! I had to walk over to Michael and sit down to talk to him.

Even then, I was unimpressed.

So why did I give him my phone number, you ask? To this day, I don't know. Maybe it was some ego trip I was on. Maybe I thought I could change that surly expression to a smile. It was a challenge, I suppose. And I love challenges.

And so I tumbled headlong into the void that was Michael.

Chapter 3

The Revelation

'And where have you been?'

My tone had been playful. I wasn't afraid of him at that stage. In those days, I didn't go over his every word in my mind looking for hidden nuances. I didn't analyse everything he said for fear of him turning my response into the basis for a roaring argument. We'd only been seeing each other for a couple of months, after all. We hadn't yet developed a strong bond of friendship but he was, I thought at the time, flatteringly attentive and I was needy.

What is it that psychologists say? There are none so vulnerable as those who want to be loved? So I guess you could say I thought I was on my way to being happy, even though we were an odd couple, Michael and me. He was intense and serious. I was always trying to please and understand everyone—the right, the wrong, the good, the bad, the cruel, and the selfish. He saw everything in black and white, in absolutes, and judged quickly. I preferred colours and shades and sometimes didn't judge at all.

When he didn't answer me straight away, I turned and looked into his eyes and my smile disappeared. His dark eyes shone with anger, his face was pale and pinched and his hands clenched and unclenched at his sides. How do you describe someone who looks less than human, even deadly?

Later on, I blamed myself for his violence and angry outbursts. Don't we all? I made myself believe that I deserved it, that I had created this series of events, inexorable as an avalanche. Somehow it was *me* who fuelled his anger until he exploded. Something in *me*, not him. Something in *my* past that made me question everything and anyone who showed me even the slightest bit of affection. As ridiculous as it seems now, these beliefs were very real to me back then. So, yes, I deserved what I got.

All garbage, of course. Real victim mentality. It's obvious to me, as I look back. But I wasn't stupid so I don't know why I didn't see what was coming, or why the alarm bells in my head weren't ringing like crazy.

I remember stepping back in surprise, almost expecting his hands to shoot out at me although nothing like that had happened before. My hand flew to my mouth as I whispered, 'What's wrong?'

In a second, he'd crossed the space between us and brought his face so close to mine I could feel his breath moving the fringe of hair on my forehead. As he leant towards me, the room suddenly darkened.

I looked over towards the door and saw storm clouds racing across the sky. An omen of what was to come.

His eyes darted to his right, as if to see what I'd looked at, but then swung back. His gaze again held mine. For a moment, I thought he was going to tell me he'd lost his job or someone had run into the back of his car, something like that. The look of contempt on his face astounded me. Almost hatred.

Far fetched? Maybe. But I don't know how to describe that moment. I knew instantly he was someone I couldn't reason with. A predatory animal almost. Someone whose mind was incapable of normal human emotion. And this made him dangerous.

But I'm racing ahead of myself because this feeling was so fleeting. It was there one second and gone the next. All I was aware of was that something had changed this man, a man I thought I knew into... I don't know what. A stranger. An alien. It was enough for me to hold my breath as he spoke.

'Don't you *ever* talk to me like that again.'

Spittle sprayed from his mouth. I could see droplets moving slowly in the air, almost suspended, as they made their way towards my face.

'Don't you *dare* treat me like one of your bloody children!'

I could see the muscles beneath his shirt rigid with anger and, as I looked at him, I saw him as if in reverse in a film negative—where everything was the same but different. I knew this man but I didn't. The concept of what I thought him to be had disappeared, replaced by this malevolent substitute.

Something—an instinct—told me not to answer him. What would I have said anyway? I forced myself to look away; I *tore* my eyes away, back to the dishes I'd been washing, only then realising I'd been holding my breath. I could feel the anger coming from him in waves. It took all of my strength not to run from him and put a locked door between us. But not with my two children sitting quietly in the loungeroom watching 'The Simpsons'. And, at that stage, I had nothing on which to base my fears— except the sudden urge to flee. Nothing concrete. He'd never hurt me before.

I always try to lighten tense moments. I hate tension, always have, so I was tempted to turn around and force a smile on my face and punch him lightly on the arm while saying something witty or silly. Make his anger go away. But what could I say to someone who was barely holding himself together?

I couldn't even trust my voice to come out in anything except a croak indicating my fear.

So, fighting to keep my voice even, I said, 'We've already eaten but I have leftovers if you'd like some.' Sweet as honey. The heroine in a movie. A real convent girl.

He didn't answer for a moment but, in my peripheral vision, I saw his shoulders slump as he stared broodily at my right shoulder. I wanted to ask if he was all right. I even began rehearsing how I would start and began to play over a little scene in my mind, when he suddenly turned and walked away, heading towards the bathroom.

'Hey,' I turned around and managed to say to his back, 'You want a glass of wine?'

I kept my voice soft. I wanted to know what had caused this extreme reaction but decided not to push it. I didn't want to know what minor mishap had changed him into this *being.* It was easier just to blame myself for pushing him in this direction. Easier to say it was my insensitive question at the end of a long day.

Unfortunately, low self-esteem has always been my problem. I had no sense of self-worth, which made me a sitting duck for anybody with a kind word. You probably know women like that. Emotionally dependent. In those days, I always had to be the agreeable one; never the one to say no. Everyone had to like me. I couldn't stand to be disliked. Instead, I was the one to adjust, to change. In actual fact, this was my weakness but, instead, I saw it as my strength.

He gave the wall an abrupt nod and said in a strangely hollow voice, 'Yeah,' before slowly undoing his tie and turning back to me.

'What happened?' I wanted to ask but changed my mind. I nodded. 'Okay' was all I said. Then, 'How was your day?'

'Fucking *drop* it, will you!' he snapped.

His outburst made me jump—this time in surprise.

'All right,' I said, my tone halfway between conciliatory and annoyed. 'I was only asking.'

'Then don't, you stupid...' His voice choked off as he snatched up his tie and stormed out of the house onto the veranda.

What would my life have been like if I hadn't been stupid enough to run after him? But I didn't think about that, or I'd never have gone out of the house. So instead, I ran after him. I caught up to him and grabbed his arm.

'Michael, please. Talk to me. What have I done wrong? What's happened?'

Then he did a scary thing. He slowly turned to me and began jabbing me, about five times, in the chest. It's amazing how much just one finger can hurt. If done hard enough, each jab leaves little round bruises between your breasts for days afterwards. With each jab, he said, 'Go (jab) away (jab) and leave (jab) me (jab) alone (jab).' His mouth was set in a rigid line as he stared down at the angry red circles on my chest.

I pushed his hand away and yelled. '*You* go away. Go on. Leave!'

His eyes jerked up and he looked at me, all anger suddenly gone. They seemed to glaze over and became blank and staring. At first no sound came out but then he murmured, 'I'm not good enough for you. I don't deserve you.'

Before I could say a word, he crossed over to a table and chairs in the corner of the veranda and sat down. His hands hung between his legs and his head dropped forward forlornly, chin on chest.

What was I to do after a statement like that? I glanced over towards the door to see if my boys had heard the commotion and come out to see what was going on. Nothing.

It's odd, I suppose, that when I think back over all that happened at that terrible time, little unconnected memories are the first things that spring to mind. The long, beautiful summer. The almost inaudible creak of the wooden swing in the yard. The maple tree in my front yard dropping its fiery red leaves on my lawn. The weather had been glorious. But then, I did live in Brisbane.

It's surprising the things you remember. I remember thousands of tiny sand flies hovering around the outside light like a grey cloud. A few drops of rain falling onto the leaves of the Leopard tree that I kept promising myself to trim back before it took over the yard. I could hear the leaves rustling. The sorrowful barking of a dog. A baby crying in the distance.

It seemed that Queensland let go of its grip on summer reluctantly. It was only weeks away from what was officially winter but, in the mornings, the sun still had a gentle warmth even if the sea breeze had picked up the oncoming chill. What never ceases to amaze me are the magnificent blue skies and the endless starry nights. This day, however, had been only a series of sunny breaks. A gust of wind moved across the lawn, rippling through the grass like the muscles of an animal. Now, under the heavy sky, afternoon had moved into night and I saw lightning flicker through the neighbour's fig tree. I could see a patch of pansies I'd planted glowing like droplets of fire in the dusk.

I looked back at him. He was staring off into the distance, the whites of his eyes shining in the half-darkness, taking no notice of me. All I could hear was the buzzing of insects and my heart beating. He'd lost more weight of late and the shadows gave his face a corpse-like look. He opened his mouth but all I could see was darkness.

'Are you going to tell me what's wrong?' I said the words more bravely than I felt. I was anxious for him to leave but I wanted him to justify his outburst to me. I waited but he was silent.

'Michael?' I repeated.

'We used to play together all the time,' he began. 'When it snowed, our mother would collapse card-board boxes and place them on the ground and we would imagine we were on sleds.'

If the roof had suddenly fallen in, I doubt if he would have noticed. In the warmth of April in Brisbane, I shivered and told myself it was the oncoming rain. Michael's story had made him oblivious to his surroundings and I had no wish to stop him talking. His tone was flat and his body motionless.

He'd never told me anything about his childhood back in Birmingham, always saying that it was history and we should concentrate on the future. These two sentences told me that he'd had a sibling—a sister or a brother, I wasn't sure which.

'One day, after a particularly heavy downfall, we were told that we wouldn't be going to school; it was closed because of the snow, and we were to stay inside and play quietly. I wanted to go outside and play, desperately wanted to, but I sulked in my room instead, while Thomas stayed in his.

'Thomas was two years older than me, nine years old at the time, and he was my hero. If he said the sky was green, I would have believed him. He was the favourite. I thought so anyway. He always got the new clothes and I always got his hand-me-downs. Mother always laughed at his antics while mine always ended up in something being broken. He always got a terrific report card while I struggled to pass most subjects. But still I loved him.

'This day, I looked out of my window, down towards the front step that led onto the footpath and the road beyond. And there he was, sitting on a sheet of cardboard in the snow while I was sitting in my room. It sounds silly now, but I was only seven and it seemed so unfair that he was doing what I'd been wanting to do all along. It sent me into a temper. I ran to my closet and took out my cardboard sheet, panting with anger. I ran all the way down the stairs, and flung open the front door. I stood there for a few seconds to see if he had the gall to turn around and apologise for excluding me, scared to go outside because I'd been told not to but determined not to miss out on any of the fun either. I could see snow covering the steps so that their shape was gone and, in my imagination, it looked like a ski-slope. Thomas was sitting on his sheet of cardboard but at the sound of the door opening, he turned around and smiled at me. Anger filled me. I put my cardboard down behind him, sat down and kicked his back with all of my might.

'The pressure of my feet plus the smooth surface of snow sent him down the steps, out of control. He reached the bottom but continued onwards across the slippery footpath and onto the road.'

I gasped. I couldn't help it because I knew what was coming. I was mesmerised by his story. Michael, of course, didn't even register my reaction. He wasn't here. He was back thirty years ago when he was seven years old and about to relive an ordeal that he would never forget for the rest of his life.

'Thomas didn't see the car coming. He was concentrating on where he was going and holding onto the cardboard. But I saw the car. I saw the eyes of the driver open wide in alarm as Thomas flew out from the footpath into the path of his car. He had no chance of stopping, of course. None whatsoever. And neither did Thomas.'

Michael sighed and shifted uncomfortably in his seat as if to indicate that the story was over. 'I nearly killed my brother that day. Thomas was in hospital for twelve months after that and he has never walked since.' He stood up and sighed again. 'And I was sent to boarding school at the end of the school term for the next eleven years. Thomas hasn't spoken to me since I was twelve.'

He glanced over at me. 'Today is his birthday. I had to make you understand, but it's not easy.' He sighed. 'You're so formidable, you know. Aloof. Almost arrogant.'

Me? I was shocked at his picture of me. I knew I was an elusive person, secretive by nature, but arrogant? No! Aloof? Perhaps. Reserved, yes. Sometimes weary, tired of insincerity and triviality and unwitting cruelty, which was a throwback to my days with foster parents. But he'd seen me as something else.

Cold. And that wasn't me at all. Defensive was probably more like it.

Why should I care what he thought, you ask? After all, I'd only just started seeing him. Now, all these years later I have the luxury of saying, 'If only I'd been like Rhett Butler, never giving a damn, I'd have saved myself a lot of pain and sorrow'. But I didn't want to be hard. I didn't want to be encased in an impervious shell and I didn't want to be arrogant.

'You've never been afraid that everything could come apart,' he continued.

I breathed in the air through my mouth.

Never been afraid... I didn't look at him. I wasn't seeing him. I was seeing myself as an eight-year-old, abandoned and feeling so disposable, as my father sadly walked away from me, leaving me once more in the hands of the nuns at Nazareth House.

Never been afraid... And the emptiness that enveloped me, cold as a shroud, when I realised I'd never see my mother again. I was too young to remember much about my mother before she abandoned me to the nun's care in the orphanage so she remains an odd, shadowy collection of smells and impressions. In my teens, I used to search the crowds hoping to catch a glimpse of someone I could associate with her, something in a stranger's face. Those moments soon passed but I remember the fear when I realised she was lost to me.

Never been afraid… sure!

We faced each other, each of us quite alone.

'I know how it feels to be afraid,' I said softly. Yes, I knew. I knew how it was when life felt like being in a small boat caught in huge waves with everything on deck slipping and sliding. Knew what it felt like to be just one scared child among fifty others crying out for attention and acceptance.

'Now you know my big secret. Conversation stopper, wouldn't you say?' There was utter desolation in his voice.

So, I walked over to him and put my arms around him. 'Oh Michael,' I whispered. 'Oh Michael.'

The next morning before leaving for work, I called his flat but there was no answer.

Since leaving Pizza Hut two months earlier, I had been lucky enough to walk into a casual job with a paint company in an industrial area of Acacia Ridge. While the work was tedious and unexciting, it paid the bills. Barely. It also meant that I could drop the boys off at school before eight o'clock in the morning and pick them up at three o'clock afterwards. Although their arrival at such an early hour wasn't exactly pleasing to me, I had no other choice: it was a thirty-five minute drive to start work at 8.30 a.m. It meant driving like a maniac to be there on time and leaving at 2.30 p.m., repeating the crazy process to be back in time to pick up the boys after school.

I admit I was disappointed when there was no answer and resentful that he wasn't there waiting for my call when I was so caught up in this new role of friend and confidante.

I let it go another day then called again, frustrated that I couldn't contact him and that he hadn't thought to contact me. Maybe he'd been busy and just hadn't had the time to call. If that was the case, I reasoned, I *should* be pleased that he'd managed to forget the ordeal he'd told me about and begin to repair his life. I *should* have, but instead I found myself being a little offended. What did that say about me? Was I self-centred? Was I clingy? I didn't think so but then again, not many of us are aware of our own faults, are we? If we were, we'd try to fix them.

What I *did* feel was that we were both damaged goods. I thought *I* was the vulnerable one but here was someone else who was just as susceptible to bruising.

I sat and brooded the next night, willing the phone to ring and finally thinking 'blow it', and went to bed.

The next day dawned clear with bright sunshine filtering through the trees that only recently had shown signs of the coming winter. I lifted my face to the sun and relished its warmth. It calmed and soothed me. The air smelled fresh and my mood lightened considerably despite what I regarded was an obvious snub from Michael.

I had an easy run to work that day, whether it was because the inevitable road works had been completed or because all the workers had decided on an early coffee break, I have no idea. Everyday it seemed, unremitting roadworks spurred on by a looming election created hellish traffic. This month it was storm-water drains, just in time for the dry season. Usually, smug men in luminous yellow vests; one man working while five others stood around watching, seemingly oblivious as the traffic formed and idled in bumper-nudging intimacy.

But whatever the reason for the respite this morning, I was grateful and sat on 75 k.p.h. the whole way.

Michael called me that day and the horror commenced.

Chapter 4

The First Time

'Talk to me, Michael.'

We were on our way back from Lewis and Sue's.

During the 'transition period' between my divorce and Michael, Sue was a friend who was closer to me than most but one I still kept, God only knows why, at a reasonable distance. She, on the other hand, had dozens of friends. We'd met when we were twenty, in our first job together. We were both shy and because of this, we bonded immediately.

I didn't have parents and her mother's home didn't feel like home anymore after her father's death. She spent all her time trying not to let her mother's problems drag her into the depths.

Even to me, Sue sounded a bit heartless but I guess, at that age, everyone is self-absorbed and selfish. Thirteen years later, with kids of our own, we still kept in touch.

This was to be the first time that my friends were going to meet Michael after three months of us seeing each other, and he hadn't been keen to go. It wasn't a good start to the evening and it created tension between us before the night even began.

'They're your friends, not mine or even ours,' he

argued petulantly before we left. 'And tell me, do you always dress like this?' He looked me up and down in a condescending way, 'Is it because you're not interested in fashion or is it because you've just got no taste?'

What was wrong with what I was wearing? I remember it was a pair of jeans and a black pullover that I thought made me look almost pretty because of the contrast of the dark material and my blond hair. As I talked to him the cloth felt scratchy and prickly against my skin. Why was it that everything I did went wrong even when I tried to do what was right? Michael always made me feel so inept and unsure. Unsure of how I lived my life. Unsure of myself. Too fearful and then not fearful enough. Everything.

There they were. The classic signs. I should have asked myself: Does he ever allow me an opinion? Does he talk down to me? Is he a loner? Does he have problems at work? Does his need for me create an attraction? Does he have trouble controlling his anger? If I'd seen the signs and asked myself these questions, everything would have been different. Actually, I *had* seen the signs but I hadn't put them in the right category and when I did it was too late. I had allowed him to be fully ensconced in my life by then, like some tick under my skin or a mosquito in my ear.

Before we even left for the party, my stomach had become a knot of trepidation. I had no wish to be embarrassed by trying to placate my sulky new partner, even if it was at my oldest friend's house.

'But they could be our friends,' I said, dismissing his caustic remark and wondering who *his* friends actually were because I'd never seen any. 'I've wanted you to meet them for weeks. I want my friends to be yours and vice versa.'

'So I can sit there and have them appraise me like a prize monkey.'

'They're not going to appraise you. It's a party, for goodness sake. You're being ridiculous.'

It was one month past the 'revelation' as I called it to myself, and we were still finding out things about each other. Every now and then, I'd tried bringing up the incident but he always brushed it aside, saying it wasn't important.

Except it was. To me anyway. What happened that night created a presence between us and I thought we needed to talk about it. It obviously still preyed on his mind from time to time—like a slow release poison.

Later on, I blamed myself for what happened after the party, reasoning that I had handled it badly. It's only now that I realise his predisposition for violence was *his* problem not mine.

His head made a small darting turn to look at me after my 'ridiculous' statement, and the consoling smile that was rising on my lips disappeared when I saw the look in his eyes. It was enough to make me suck in a surprised breath until he spoke again.

'Don't treat me like an imbecile,' he said quietly. Menacingly. I watched his jaw clench and unclench so I shut up and said nothing more on the subject. Somewhere in the recesses of my mind, I sensed that Michael, already angry, would neither listen nor believe me while he was in this mood.

'And what is it with you Australians anyway? Someone asks you to a barbecue and you take drinks, food, the lot. In England, you throw a party and it means just that. *You* throw the party. You don't expect it to be a BYO *everything*.'

He was one of the few people I've known who, despite cloudless skies and brilliant sunshine, hated barbecues. When most people enjoy grabbing a bottle of wine and a bowl of salad to take to a friend's house for a sit-around-the-barbecue, Michael much preferred going to a pub and watching football on the TV; rain, hail or shine.

I wanted to tell him to stop being so pathetic, to stop acting like a spoilt child but I couldn't actually bring myself to say the words. The thing was that, even at this early stage, I was wary of this man, as unfortunately I'm wary of most men now. Oh, I know it was apparent that he just didn't want to go and was throwing a tantrum actually. I was also aware of his open aggression towards my friends. But despite my uncomfortable feeling, I shrugged and let his comments ride.

In spite of the shaky beginning, the night went well, or so I thought. Michael put on his James Dean persona again and said very little but I put that down to first-meeting jitters. On the way home, his mood grew darker.

'Are you okay?' I asked, feeling quite light-headed and contented.

He just stared out the taxi window. I could see he was angry but I had no idea why.

'Michael?' I murmured quietly so that the taxi driver couldn't hear what was being said. 'What's wrong?' I asked as I leaned towards him and touched his arm.

He mumbled something as he wrenched his arm away from me.

'Pardon?' I asked. There was no response. 'I'm sorry. I didn't hear what you said.'

He looked at me and I could see him trying to control his anger. 'Nothing,' he said between gritted teeth.

'Something's wrong,' I persisted. 'Have I done something wrong?'

Why hadn't I just shut up?

'Don't tell me you don't know.'

'But I don't. I really don't.'

He stared at me with such contempt I squirmed a little in my seat. He had this habit of tilting his head to the side when he was considering what he would say. So, he gave me his tilt and said 'Crap,' through clenched teeth before turning away again.

The word hung in the air like the sound of a slap and I could have sworn my scalp receded against my skull. Warning enough? Not for me. I was shocked at the vehemence in his voice. All the words I had inside to compromise evaporated before they were spoken. I wasn't so drunk that I didn't know what I'd said or done. As far as I knew, I'd behaved well. I'd paid Michael attention all night, introducing him to whoever I knew. I'd included him in all the jokes told. I'd only had three drinks so I was aware of everything that had happened. Michael wasn't Lewis's cup of tea, but to give Lewis his due, he gave Michael his best shot. Good food, lots of good wine and good company. What could have gone wrong?

He refused to talk to me so when the cab pulled up in front of my house, I asked, 'Are you coming in or are you just going home?'

He got out of the cab and threw $10 on the front seat of the cab, half the fare I noticed, and walked towards my house.

Now I was starting to get angry and, if it wasn't for the cab driver, I would have yelled at him then and there. I handed the driver another $10 and thanked him before following Michael up the front stairs.

'What the hell's going on?' I shouted at him. I was more than a little piqued that he was treating my house like it was his own. I'd never been to his flat— even though I'd hinted several times that I had no idea where he lived—so watching him walk confidently up to my front door really got my back up.

He stood back silently as I unlocked the front door. I walked in, thanking God that it was my ex-husband's weekend to have the boys. I had no wish for them to see Michael in this mood.

I turned to face him. 'Michael, this is mad. If I've done something wrong, just tell me.'

He turned to me then with a look on his face that would become all too familiar to me in the next months. Contempt mixed with frightening anger.

'Are you stupid or what?'

I could feel the anger building up inside me. 'No, I don't think so,' I said breathing slowing to control myself. 'But if I've done something wrong, I'm sorry.'

I waited for him to answer. I shrugged. Waited again.

'I hate being made a fool of,' he said. 'You made me feel unimportant in front of your friends.'

I gaped at him. 'I did? When did I do that?' I honestly didn't know.

He went into the parody of a conversation. 'Michael doesn't work for Pizza Hut anymore. He works for a company selling vacuum cleaners now,' he said in a falsetto voice.

Then the realisation dawned on me. I *had* said that, but it was a part of a much bigger conversation.

We'd talked about how difficult it was to find work these days if you didn't want to do shift work. I had found it hard to find decent work after I left Pizza Hut, and then only part-time, so having enough money to pay the bills was hard enough, much less having any spare cash for luxuries. I'd gone on to say that Michael had left Pizza Hut too.

I almost laughed. *That was it?*

'Oh come on. You've got to be joking. That's why you're angry? Everyone knows how tough it is to find work these days.'

He said nothing. Just stared at me, his eyes deadpan.

'I'm sorry, Michael. I didn't mean it to be derogatory. I was just stating a fact. It was probably insensitive of me but I meant nothing by it.' I knew how hard it had been for him to make the transition from a Pizza Hut manager to a low-grade salesman, and maybe it was those three drinks that had made me relax my guard, but I honestly hadn't meant to hurt his feelings. 'I'll make us some coffee.'

I felt bad for having upset him but at the same time I knew it wasn't anything that was too awful although, as I walked into the kitchen and filled the jug with water, I began to remember with an uneasy feeling, snippets of the conversation that night.

Lewis to me: '... remember the time when...'

Sue to Lewis: '...you always were a show off...'

Me to Sue: '...this trifle is marvellous...'

But not a word from or to Michael.

It was only then that I sensed him behind me as I pushed the 'on' button of the kettle and began to reach for two coffee mugs. Positive that he was coming over to make up, I half-turned towards him with a smile on my face. Then I saw something flying towards me. I had no time to put my hands up to protect my face before something connected solidly with my cheek bone.

Pain exploded inside my head and I went down like a ton of bricks. I remember thinking I'd hit my head on the overhead cupboard as I put my hand out to stop myself from falling hard. Either that, or something had fallen on top of my head. I even remember hearing the sounds of bees buzzing in the vortex around me, like an electrical short in the rain.

When I looked up through the haze of stars, I saw Michael looming over me. I put out my hand thinking he was there to help me up. That's when he hit me again.

My lip burst like a ripe tomato and I felt pain in

every cell of my brain. I have an idea I tried to move away from him and I think I shrieked in surprise. Brilliant light flooded my eyes and I realised he'd walked away because the glare of the kitchen light was piercing my vision.

After the initial shock, I felt a terrible bleakness. I lay there for a while, pierced and wounded, my heart racing, not sure of what had happened.

It was the end. It had to be. I'd always vowed that if any man hit me, I'd end the relationship instantly. No questions. No apology. No turning back.

Even when I'd spoken those words to friends, I'd never really thought it would happen to me. I thought I had more sense than to start a relationship with someone who was capable of hurting me. If I met a man like that, I would know immediately what sort of man he was.

But I hadn't. And there had been no warning except for that minor hint one month ago, after his 'revelation'. This had come out of the blue, with amazing suddenness. He had brought violence into my home and the result was shocking and devastating to me. What were the rules now?

I pulled myself up into a sitting position, a huge effort of will, tasting blood in my mouth. My face felt heavy and I ran my tongue over my teeth gingerly to see if any had been loosened. Everything seemed fine. I was lucky. Ha! Lucky!

I looked down at my pullover and saw blood from my lip. My head swam, so I leant back against the cupboards, feeling sick with every throb of pain in my head. *Had he left?*

I strained my ears for sounds but could hear nothing. *Good. He's gone. He's saved me the trouble of telling him to leave.* Even as the words formed in my head, I knew I was too scared to say those words to him.

I dragged myself to my feet and grabbed a tea-towel from the bench to catch any blood dripping from my mouth. Hunched over, I made my way to the bathroom and looked in the mirror. I was relieved to see that I didn't look as bad as I felt. A split lip and a swollen cheek. A cold compress would reduce the swelling on the side of my head, although I could see a bruise forming, and the lip looked only a little worse than when I had a cold sore. I spat and noticed there was blood in my saliva.

I washed my face gently and dried it, noticing that the bleeding had almost stopped. As I walked out of the bathroom, I heard a muffled sobbing from the veranda.

I should have been pleased to hear that sound. I was sure it was for my benefit. It should have made me stronger, but it didn't. What I felt was something deep inside me that said I couldn't walk away from someone who was so unhappy. A type of pity probably.

I walked outside and stood watching him for a moment. He was sitting in the same chair he had sat in one month ago, in the very same position, head bent with his hands dangling between his legs. He looked up at me, stricken.

'Trish. Oh God. I'm sorry.'

My voice was thick. 'You hit me.'

His shoulders shook in the darkness and I heard the sobs again. 'How can you ever forgive me?'

'I don't know if I can.' My voice had gained some semblance of control.

'I'm so sorry.' I remember him saying each word clearly. I remember a lightning flash at that exact moment and waiting for the thunder to follow. I remember hearing the soft ping of raindrops on the tin roof. I remember everything.

He started to cry softly again. 'I lost control. I thought everyone was making fun of me. It's not a good enough excuse, I know. I'm so ashamed of myself. I'll never do it again. I promise. I can't live without you, Trish.'

So many of us complain that men run away from commitment, so to find one so utterly devoted seemed too good to be true. To have a relationship with someone who appeared to want no-one but me signified that I may just have attained that female romantic ideal of getting and keeping my man, even if the attention was overpowering. Like millions of other innocent girls throughout the last fifty years, when I hit puberty I fell in love with novels like *Wuthering Heights*, *Rebecca* and *Gone with the Wind*. I wanted to be someone just like Cathy out of *Wuthering Heights*, loved by men like Edgar and Heathcliff, and living rather melodramatically ever after. Of course, being rich, beautiful and endlessly resourceful, not to mention triumphing over adversity, held my attention as well—and, of course, lots of stories have feisty heroines, don't they? But what had special meaning to me was perhaps the proximity of love and that passionate attachment to Cathy by the men in her life.

The extent of men's passion for us is nearly always seen by women, initially anyhow, as proof positive of female desirability and male devotion. We start out believing that this must be evidence of the perfect relationship. They cannot live without us, they want to be with us as much as possible, they have eyes for no-one else, they cherish every part of our being.

And so I went over to him.

I know. Bloody idiot! What I didn't know at that stage was that apparent devotion is often really just there to disguise jealous possessiveness: so often leading to domineering, controlling violence and then abuse. But I went over and made mother-hen noises as if he were the one with blood all over his clothes and bees buzzing around inside his head. He cried and I felt sorry for him, when I really only wanted someone to feel sorry for *me*.

What I should have been was angry. Angry that he had used me as his punching bag. Angry that he had such little regard for me. But instead, I doubted myself. I blamed myself for releasing this demon. Yet again.

'I'm not good enough for you,' he whimpered. 'I don't deserve you. I'm such a shit.'

Deep inside I wanted to agree with him but seeing him so full of repentance, I was compelled to let it go. I didn't tell him it was all right, because it wasn't, but I foolishly thought this was a breakthrough for us. It was like someone softly calling 'Cathy' across the moors.

In a way, I thought that his explanation may be true in some way. Any explanation was better than nothing at all so I grabbed it.

Maybe I had drunk too much. Maybe I had humiliated him and just couldn't remember. Rationalising, it's called. Making excuses for Michael was what it actually was. It was like I had two people in my head talking to me. One was saying, 'If you don't run, you're crazy.' The other was saying 'Talk to him. Find out what caused his anger.' As I stood there looking at him, pity was the only emotion that I had the energy to summon. So stupidly, I gave in.

It's amazing how wrong you can be. I'd actually turned into one of the stars from the soapies that I scoffed at for being foolish and blind.

Chapter 5

Kelly's Story

I watched the young girl fumbling in her purse for change, her eyes still not meeting mine.

As I wrapped up the sandwich, I asked softly, 'Are you all right?'

Once, I would have kept my mouth shut and minded my own business but I couldn't this time. I suppose you could say, she reminded me of *me* just a few months earlier.

Her eyes darted up, and then dropped to her shoes again.

'I'm fine,' she said.

'Would you like a cup of tea?'

She looked up me then shook her head.

'On the house.' I smiled. 'I could use one myself. If you don't mind sitting with me, that is.'

I saw her hesitate but then she nodded slowly and walked over to a table by the side of the front counter while I turned and made the tea. I had no idea what I was going to say to her but from experience, I knew it was good for her to talk to someone even if it meant knowing that you weren't alone in your nightmare.

As I put her cup in front of her, I said, 'My name's Trish.'

'Mine's Kelly.'

There was a little uncomfortable silence so I plunged right in. 'What happened, Kelly?'

She sighed and sat up straight for a minute, pulling her shoulders back as if working out a kink in her back, before talking.

I could see the lies forming. *I walked into a door. I tripped.* Any excuse to hide the awful truth.

Instead she said, 'Can't you tell?' She spoke a little defensively but immediately said, 'Sorry. I didn't mean to sound rude. I just don't know what to do anymore.'

She shrugged unhappily. 'He isn't always like this. He can be so wonderful when he wants to be but he gets so jealous. Sometimes all I have to do is look sideways at a man and he assumes I'm making eyes at him.' She shook her head vehemently. 'But I'm not. I love my husband.'

'Has he hit you before?'

'No. This is the first time and it was over nothing. I walked into the house yesterday afternoon after doing a little grocery shopping. I was planning a really lovely dinner, you know? His favourite. Anyway, I walked in with the shopping bags and heard the phone ringing. More and more lately, Jason has started ringing during the day wanting to know where I've been, who I've seen, how long I've been out. That sort of thing. So I knew it was him.

'I literally dropped everything at the door and ran to pick up the phone. Straight away he said, "Where have you been?" Just like that. No 'hello'. No 'how are you'. Just the grilling. So I told him. "I was out shopping." I tried to sound happy and I prattled on about how I was going to be busy for the rest of the afternoon making his favourite meal. He seemed pleased and hung up. But then, when I went back to the door to get the shopping bags, one of the jars in a bag had broken. The most important one, you know? I needed that ingredient for the meal.'

While she talked, she took tiny sips of tea. Her brow puckered from time to time and I could see it hurt her lip when she put the cup up to her mouth.

'So,' she continued. 'I raced back out to the shops to replace it. I didn't want to annoy him anymore than he already was by not having the meal prepared after I'd told him I was making it. Anyway, as I walked back in to the house, the phone was ringing again but it stopped before I could answer it. I just stood staring at it. Was it Jason? Who else could it be? Should I ring him back to see if it was him? He'd know I was home then. But if it wasn't him calling, would he be angry with me? All of these thoughts ran through my mind at the same time. I just didn't know what to do.' She shrugged. 'So I didn't do anything.'

She dropped her head, staring at the cup of tea in front of her as if she could read the future in the milky surface. A car with a blown muffler drove noisily past the shop and continued over the railway line out of sight. Distant thunder rumbled and I thought I saw a flicker of lightning in the darkening sky.

Kelly saw and heard nothing.

'Of course, it was him calling,' she said to the teacup. 'That was last night.'

'You should go to someone for help,' I said. Was I actually giving this woman advice on how to deal with a domestic violence bout? 'What about your parents?'

'I don't want my parents to know what's happening. My parents are farmers who live in a close-knit community. They just wouldn't understand. Even though they were pretty strict, there was never any violence in my childhood, which is why this is such a shock to me. I've never encountered anything like this before.'

'Maybe that's what you need now. The love of your family around you.'

'I can't go back.' She was shaking her head vehemently. 'I was pretty rebellious when I was at home. I hated living on the farm in the last couple of years; I told them that I'd be happy when I moved away. All my friends were leaving to come to Brisbane and more and more I found myself alone. I wanted to be anywhere but on a farm. I feel so bad now because it really upset Mum and I disappointed Dad.'

'Dad didn't approve of Jason from the beginning because he was seven years older than me and because he had 'airs and graces' and was a 'smooth talker'. When I left to marry Jason, I told them that they'd be sorry for the way they treated him but more and more lately I think they were right.'

'In what way?'

'Just little things. Jason didn't want me to get a job. You know, he wanted a wife to be there when he got home. And I was happy to do the wifey things: baking my own bread and biscuits, washing and ironing his shirts, having his meal on the table when he came home. I loved it because it was my way of showing him how much I cared for him.

'But lately, things have been slowly changing. He rings me a dozen times during the day for no reason at all. I used to think that he was making sure I was all right and it made me feel kind of loved but now I know it was just to check on me. And then when he comes home he says things like, 'These biscuits are soft' or 'You haven't ironed my shirts properly.' So I re-iron them again. And he said I was frigid. So I said to him, "How can I be warm and loving towards you when you're not warm and loving towards me?"

'At first, I thought it was my fault when things went wrong and he got angry at me. But then very quickly everything was my fault. It was my fault I upset him. My fault for nagging. I've been trying everything to try and keep the relationship going. But nothing seems to be working. And now there's this.'

She pointed to her split lip. Almost immediately, as if aware of what she'd told me, a total stranger, she said, 'Of course, he was sorry afterwards. And he promised it would never happen again.' Then her shoulders drooped once more. 'But I'm having trouble getting over this. You know?' Her eyes looked up pleadingly at me.

Oh, I knew. I knew only too well. Knew how the mistreatment can wear you down and cause you to lose all sense of self-worth and self-confidence. Knew how the pressure and tension built up over time until eventually there was an explosion of words and fists. Knew about the regrets and promises afterwards.

As she was speaking, I couldn't help seeing the similarities between her situation now and mine not so long ago.

Chapter 6

The Whirlpool Begins

My life was changing and I remember expecting to see the outside world changing too.

Instead, the next day was like every other day. I could smell the cut grass from someone's recently mowed lawn. Two bikes still lay on the front lawn from the day before where the boys had left them even though I continually told them not to. Everything was the same but now it was different and I didn't know how to bring it back to the way it had been only three months ago. I'd entered the relationship expecting it to develop healthily and was surprised at where I found myself.

I remembered an adage from my teens, 'When a fox hears a rabbit screaming, it comes running... but not to help'. For years it's stuck in my mind because as it turned out, I was Michael's rabbit and he was that fox.

I've often wondered why I let things go as far as I did, even though it wasn't anything I did consciously. I'd read horror stories of women who end up with burn scars, broken limbs and dead children and like everyone else, I thought, 'That'll never happen to me.' But before you even realise it, you're a statistic with no way out that you can see, living in a nightmare. There isn't one day that goes by that I don't have in my mouth the harsh taste of regret.

What I've told you already—the night with Michael on the veranda and the party at Sue and Lewis's—happened ten years ago. It's now the end of March and it's getting cooler just like it was that April night so long ago. The days grow shorter and the nights grow longer. The first chill is in the evening air. All my zygocactus are budding and the leaves of trees are turning red and falling, just like they were on that night.

At the time, I was so flattered that of all people Michael chose *me* to tell his dreadful secret: a tragic accident with tragic consequences that he always blamed himself for. So I kept quiet about my situation. I didn't want the few friends I had to see me as less than perfect. I went through terrible agonies to keep the truth to myself and away from others. I focused on what other people would think of *me* instead of focusing on Michael's lack of respect and control.

I already thought of myself as a failure. I'd only been separated for six months and here I was in a worse situation than I'd escaped from. I even imagined my friends putting two and two together and blaming me for the break-up of my marriage. And I didn't want to be like some single women: divorced and bitter. In the end, if you can believe it, it was easier to justify Michael's actions than to admit I'd made yet another mistake. After all, don't the psychologists say that no-one is born evil; they are simply moulded by their experiences?

I suppose shame kept me quiet although, as I look back now, I don't exactly know what it was I was ashamed of. Sometimes, too often perhaps, we refuse to put our fears into words because the words will make them concrete, inescapable and over-whelming. For some of us, the fear of naming also includes the fear that we will have to do something about the abuse once we admit its happening. I don't remember being conscious of this, but I sus-pect it was there. Contemplating any kind of a change was frightening for me.

I felt confused most of the time. And Michael con-fused me. Most times, I didn't know what he was going to do next. Mostly, he was like everyone else, then he'd do something perverse, like hiding my car keys for the fun of it. I never had a sense of what he would do or why he would do it. I couldn't see how his sense of cause and effect operated. He was like the surface of a lake. Something was stirring below but I didn't know what.

It seemed easy to find myself in this situation but not so easy to find my way out again. I guess, even at that stage, I realised that most people have no sympathy for a woman who stays with an abusive man and I didn't want to wear that label. After all, we don't live in a part of the world where fathers sell women off to their husbands and where they have no way to survive on their own.

It seemed finding out *why* I let this happen to me was just as important as finding the fix and I made myself think seriously about it. Two things kept coming back. One was the message I received in the orphanage. We were brought up to be seen and not heard. They didn't allow us to have our own opinions or to make our own choices. Everyone else's feelings came first and, in any case, other people— especially the nuns—always knew better. Some version of this message was received and translated into the belief that if our feelings counted at all, they came last and that other people knew what was best for us, better than we did ourselves. In the nun's defence, I'd say they did their best and, through ignorance and lack of understanding, presented only an extreme version of the attitudes of the day.

Not only did this undermine my self-assurance, it made me feel as if I didn't exist at all. I was brought up without a sense of self-worth or individual identity, and without the skills or the confidence to make decisions or the means to stand up for myself. If I'd been able to stand up just once and voice my inner feelings, then I might have been able to stand up to Michael.

The second thing that came to me was the circumstances of my marriage. Besides the fact that I'd married far too young, without experiencing life in any shape or form, I also remembered that my overwhelming emotion at that time was one of surprise, surprise that someone, anyone, would actually want *me*. After all, no-one else had, I thought when I remembered the many times I'd been delivered back to the orphanage by so many different foster parents. So, to stop that pattern of being 'thrown back' yet again, I tried to mould myself to be what my husband wanted me to be. *Willing* myself to be the perfect wife. With no basis for comparison, I made myself subservient, obedient and unobtrusive, yet aware of his every need. The problem with that, of course, is that I lost sight of my own needs—and so did he.

When Mother's Day came one year, he played golf with his friends, leaving me at home with our two-year-old while I was six months pregnant with our second child. When I found myself in the finals of a squash competition, he said he needed the car to play tennis with a friend of his, leaving me at home unable to attend the finals and therefore forfeiting. When he came into the hospital room, four hours after my second baby was born, the first words he spoke to me were, 'You'd better do your exercises. Your tummy looks flabby.' Although the pain certainly registered, I still accepted this behaviour.

The truth was I'd allowed my ex-husband to dominate me. And I allowed Michael to take over where my ex-husband left off and move on to new heights.

One factor I've found that keeps women under the control of these men is that they're scared. Another is they have very little self-confidence. And that was me in a nutshell. When my husband and I separated, I was still shy and suspicious of strangers and making friends had always been difficult—even though to those who know me now, this may sound surprising. These days, I'm not confrontational but I like to think that I am assertive.

So how could I accept Michael's dreadful behaviour? It took me many years to ask myself the same question, but when I did, the answer came quickly and succinctly: because I thought it was *my* fault.

In the months that followed, I sometimes lay awake listening as the moths hit themselves against the flyscreen, smashing their wings as they tried to reach the light. Why would they destroy themselves in order to fly towards a bright white orb that would kill them anyway? When I had those thoughts,

I covered my head with my sheet because I didn't want to know the answer. I knew I was no better than those stupid moths.

Everything began to accelerate downhill after that party at Sue and Lewis's. Michael changed overnight, it seemed. His moods moved between an exhilarating high one day and an unhappy dangerous low the next. He began to rifle through my drawers and read my diary to know where I would be on any given day. I would have to tell him exactly where I had been when I was away from him. He even checked the mileage of my car after I'd used it.

And then there was the amount of milk in his coffee, what I wore, how I did my hair, his impatience towards me and the amount of alcohol he drank... all utterly ludicrous reasons to assault anyone but those were the sort of excuses he used.

Why did I take it? Because I didn't know how to stop it, I suppose. And my pride wouldn't allow me to think of myself as abused because I wasn't the cowering type. I suppose it takes most women a long time to believe that someone they've chosen could turn out to be abusive. I found it hard to believe that something with so much potential could turn into *this*. Such an immensity of difference. It was like standing in a desert without shade while the hot sun beats down on you—how could this once have seemed like an oasis?

Usually the hope is that the man's behaviour is just a one-off or two-off occurrence and it will stop. But I soon found out it wasn't that easy. So I went along with it and hoped that soon he'd see what he was doing and come to his senses. It wasn't that I didn't recognise aggression and violence; rather it was that I didn't have any sense of judgement. I didn't have any ability to be critical of other people or judge them.

But I knew I was in trouble. *That* I *did* know. I had already begun to alienate most of my friends and there was no-one to help me so I learnt to know what set him off. I knew what subjects to avoid and I smiled to cover up the knots in my stomach. It was better to change myself than to fight the unfairness and suffer the consequences. I would do better next time. It was *my* fault.

It sometimes seems like our capacity for self-blame is limitless. Not only did I expect myself to be vigilant but if I slipped up even once I blamed myself. As in a storm, I could sometimes feel the tension rising, building. I began to read his moods and see warning signs appearing on the horizon:

words, glances, intimidating gestures. Sensitive to these warning signs, I got very good at avoiding the coming onslaught by staying out of the way. Well, most of the time. Even peaceful situations turned so suddenly that sometimes I was left amazed by the abruptness of his change. One minute we'd be sitting quietly watching TV and the next he'd backhand me for simply talking during it.

So, as hard as I tried, I could never escape. I even began to believe that I was lucky to have anyone want me at all.

'You can't even keep your friends,' he would say to me.

'But I do have friends,' I cried back.

'You're mad if you believe that. So tell me, where are these so-called friends?' he'd ask.

I wanted to say, 'I don't see them anymore because of you.' It was the truth, of course, but I was wise enough to know what would happen if I spoke those words. The storm would come. So I said nothing. I agreed with him until, eventually, I began to believe him.

Then, amazingly, he would smile brilliantly at me and say how wonderful I was. All the tell-tale traces of his anger—the frown, the lips pressed tightly in a harsh line—disappeared and once again, pleasure transformed his face.

Don't gag when I tell you this, but he could sparkle when he wanted to. There would be glimpses of the happiness I yearned for, like a window being opened in a sweltering room and a puff of cool air blowing in.

You see, he wasn't always violent. I suppose they never are. If he had been, it would have been easier for me to close that book. He could be charming and attentive when he wanted to be. Flatteringly so. In between bouts, he could be humorous and attentive so I saw him as a tragic figure trying to release the demons of his past. And don't forget he'd opened up his heart to *me* and told *me* his secret. To anyone who didn't know better, he was the voice of reason.

In those periods, we took the boys to their basketball games together, both of us encouraging them or commiserating with them. Michael played soccer with them in the front yard and in the backyard we had competitions to see who could throw the greatest number of basketball hoops. I would stand and watch him, wondering why he couldn't be like this all of the time.

Patronising kindness followed his cruelty and left me doubting my own sanity. I would then begin to think

I had imagined everything. That I really *was* going mad. Then, days later, lulled into thinking things had changed, I would turn and say something that would make him furious and the cycle would begin again. I remember thinking it would be wonderful to say something suddenly without testing it on my lips first but told myself that, if I tried harder and was more careful, everything would be all right.

It was during one of Michael's lulls that, as part of our 'bonding' process, he decided to teach me to play golf . He loved golf and was quite good at it, but I soon learnt the reason it was named 'golf': it was because all of the other four-letter words were taken.

To say I was hopeless is an understatement and this created more arguments because he couldn't understand how I could be so useless at it—after all, I played tennis and squash; both ball sports. But no matter how hard I tried, I lost more balls than I cared to replace and, if I counted my air swings, I could easily double my score. So, in disgust, he abandoned my lessons.

He knew my vulnerable areas. He knew my boundaries and picked away at the little confidence I had until I wasn't sure of anything anymore, making me so dependent on him that I had to ask his opinion on everything. Eventually I became quite ineffectual and that angered him as well. I just couldn't win.

More and more, depression weighed heavily on me. I was in a continual state of chaos; confused and unsure of what to do to keep the peace and unable to prevent the storms. I regard myself as intelligent but the million dollar question is why I stayed with Michael for eighteen months when we had so very little in common and when, for sixteen of those months, he was hitting me. And why was it that I protected and covered up for that violent man in my life?

The answers are complex and varied but none the less pathetic. My answer was that I'd opened up the can of worms and let them out and it was my responsibility to put them back again. You see, *I* was the wrong ingredient. The bad apple. Without me, and with someone else, wouldn't he have been a happy well-balanced person?

I can almost see you shaking your head in disbelief but, as sorry as the reasoning was, it was what I thought. Women have this automatic reflex to blame themselves and I didn't want to believe that someone I thought I could love would hurt me and would continue to do it.

In the beginning, I never saw him as cruel or violent.

I saw him as a victim of his past who, every now and then, had to release the poisons inside him in order to survive. And, outwardly, there didn't seem to be anything hostile about him. The abuse crept in slowly and subtly.

So I felt like I was walking on egg-shells, wondering each day whether he would be *normal* or whether today he would be sullen or irritable. Initially I'd thought his moods and the way he was acting were my fault but eventually, after hearing about the many girlfriends he'd had in England, I began to wonder if our relationship was following a similar path to the ones he'd had back in Birmingham.

In the beginning, he seemed genuinely pleased that I took an interest in his well-being but, as time wore on, familiarity set in and the demons were released once more. Like any new relationship, the newness of it distracted him but very soon he awarded me glimpses of his true nature and manipulation raised its ugly head.

Manipulation can be subtle. It confuses you and can even make you doubt yourself and your own sanity. Things you say are twisted and then the mind games begin. You see, the best way to control a person is to confuse them. Instead of giving you confidence in yourself, they take it away and make you doubt yourself. Control is the key word here.

Shouldn't there have been more definite signs? Something? A premonition? An overlooked chill that would have warned me of the dark time that was approaching? A time when everything would alter so my life would became a tragedy? Did I miss the signs during those first few months—or was I simply in denial? I guess I truly believed that his sensitive side would prevail and overpower this stranger who robbed me of my self-esteem and self-worth.

Sue was the only one who ever knew of my dilemma. She would look at me disbelievingly and shake her head when I showed up with bruises.

One night, a year after I'd started seeing Michael, I'd hired a baby-sitter to stay with my boys while I had a rare night out with Sue. We went to the Britannia Inn, a mock English pub in the centre of town in the Wintergarden complex. We'd grabbed ourselves a table away from the heavy beat of the band and we'd been drinking steadily for a couple of hours when she made the statement.

I sat opposite her as she said, 'I think something's wrong.'

'What do you mean? Don't you feel well?' I asked through the alcoholic fog in my head. Usually, I didn't drink much because I'd always hated the lightness it brought to my head, the cold sweat on my temples, and the way it made me want to throw up, then sleep. Lately, it was becoming my release.

She looked down at her drink miserably.

'Come on,' I prompted. 'You can't just leave it at that.'

She raised her head and looked at me. 'I think Lewis is having an affair.'

'What?' I asked stupidly. 'With who? Or is that whom?'

She shrugged and stared into her wine glass.

Realising it was up to me to keep the conversation going even though she'd started it, I said, 'Are you sure?'

'No. It's just a feeling I have.'

Trying to be helpful, I said, 'It's nothing to be ashamed of, you know. Statistics say that sixty per cent of all married men have had affairs at some time during their marriage and it survives.'

She looked at me and snapped, 'Not bloody mine!

If he thinks he can have his cake and eat it too, he's sadly mistaken.'

The vehemence in her voice sobered me and I can't say I blamed her. I'd feel the same way if I were in her shoes although I couldn't imagine Lewis ever doing something like this. I'd known him since he was nineteen and I was twenty-two and we both worked in the public service together, fifteen years ago. You get to know someone, and trust them, very well after such a long time and he just wasn't the type. I'd even introduced him to Sue. I was at their wedding and had seen them off when Lewis went into the air force. Our kids had practically grown up together. I remembered Lewis throwing balls to the kids in my backyard so it was hard for me to imagine him as anything but a family man.

I leant back and looked at her. 'What are you going to do?'

She laughed humourlessly. 'What can I do? I'm stuck with him. I've got two kids, no job and bills up to my armpits.'

I could see her mentally shake herself. 'Enough about me. How's Michael the Moron?' She'd taken to calling him that after the first couple of times I turned up with bruises. 'Why don't you get rid of him?'

I used to ask myself the same question but after that first revelation of his... I don't know. I felt sorry for him and blamed myself for being callous and insensitive. I honestly thought it was my fault for not being what he needed or what he wanted me to be. It was *me* who'd brought this out in him and it was up to *me* to get rid of it.

I knew he was capable of a kind of tenderness and he was sorry after he hit me (in the beginning, that is). But my emotions changed from day to day and nothing was ever black or white. It was the typical ambivalence of a survivor of domestic violence. They say love is blind but it can also be pathetic. It reduces us to act like idiots or the sort of people who infuriate us in soapies as we sit back and shake our heads and say, 'What a fool!'

It's not that I didn't believe in love. I did. I longed to feel the 'pangs of love'. I just never had so far and, in my mind, I thought love was something that came eventually after getting to know the other person's faults as well as their good points.

And then came the worst decision I ever made in my life.

Chapter 7

Trying to Break the Spell

It was a night like many others.

We were quietly watching an old black-and-white movie—Gregory Peck in some thriller—but its name escapes me. My boys were with their father so I'd given in to Michael's badgering and gone to his flat. I'd been there only a couple of times because I didn't really like it. Not because he didn't keep it clean but it was something in me. I never felt relaxed or at ease there. I acted like a schoolgirl sitting in front of the principal—still and uncomfortable just waiting for the worst to happen. Probably subconsciously I felt safer at my house although it didn't seem to matter when or where Michael's rages began.

So there we were, sitting in front of the TV when, suddenly, he stood up and switched it off.

'Hey! Why'd you do that?' I asked.

'I'm tired and it's a crappy movie.'

During the beginning of my 'Michael period', I had begun to censor myself. It got that bad. I'd begin to say something, at times let things slip out, and instantly regret it. I had to train myself to keep my mouth shut instead of speaking out loud. But I hated being careful of what I said and I didn't want to spend my life holding things back. It was this imbalance between saying what I wanted and keeping it bottled up that made me say, 'No, it's not. It's a classic and I want to watch it.'

'I said it's crappy and we're going to bed.'

Can you see what's coming? Yes, so could I. But by this stage, I'd been beaten and bullied so many times I was damned if I was going to trot demurely off to bed with him, just because he could hit hard or because he didn't give a fig about my needs or opinions. Fair enough? I thought so, too.

I'd been able to avoid the last few beatings he'd almost administered but not this one.

I won't go into the argument; I'll spare you the details because it was similar to and as inevitable as all of the others. Suffice to say, I ended up with Michael hitting my head on top of the TV and mushing my face into the screen.

Then he went to bed leaving me on the floor dripping blood onto the carpet from yet another cut lip.

I stood up and cleaned myself in the bathroom expecting him to come in at any time, mumbling an apology or, at least, admonishing me for not wanting to go to bed with him earlier, hence the argument. But there was nothing.

I steadied myself before walking into his bedroom. There he was, sound asleep in bed, snoring softly. The first few times he'd been remorseful but now he was just indifferent to the pain he caused me.

I watched him sleep, expecting him to sit up and see what he'd done. I wanted him to, so I could see the look in his eyes as I told him I was leaving and not coming back. I felt strong enough to do that now.

But he kept sleeping peacefully.

I wondered how I had come to be this pathetic creature, trying to make right out of what was so wrong. Could this be me? I was the one who was always so strong. Why had I let all my defences down? I felt like a child lost in a strange dream.

Gradually, I began to be realistic about Michael and me. Sure, there were highs and lows in every relationship but the highs were becoming fewer and fewer and the lows were just plain soul-destroying. Like a flash I knew our relationship had been doomed from the start and that I actually hated him. It simply fuelled my resolve to walk away. I suppose up to now what I'd felt was a strange kind of passivity at the results of his abuse. Like Olive Oyl on Prozac. But now I had to take action.

I picked up my bag, weighing it in my hand to see if

I could hit him with it hard enough while he slept. I clenched my hands and gritted my teeth while I breathed heavily; my heart pounded so hard I was sure he'd wake up.

I even thought of leaving him a note, but what would I say? Thank you for making the last six months of my life a misery? I will not miss the cruel words you utter to me about my mother being a whore and me not much better? I will not miss the tantrums and the weekly fights over nothing? In the end, I decided not to write anything at all. Without a word, I turned and left.

In my car, the tears came. Relief mingled with a sense of loss. I'd wasted six months of my life, tried so hard and the result was no different than it would have been if I'd walked away from him the night of the 'revelation'. All I'd managed to do was prolong the agony. But just as I'd done when I was fifteen, I'd taken the opportunity to close off a period of my life; the pain was like an open wound.

On the drive back, my lip throbbed and my head ached but I felt a soaring joy at my new-found resolve never to see him again. I was struck by a realisation that I'd decided once and for all to move forward with my life and have nothing more to do with Michael. It jolted me and filled me with excitement. I was going to walk away from him and leave him to sort out his own problems. I'd done it! I'd broken the spell I was under.

Suddenly I became alert, like a subject who has been under a hypnotist's spell. I'd been driving, letting my autopilot take me home. I lifted my foot off the accelerator and the car slowed down.

Chapter 8

Yet Another Mistake

Imagine being alone in a house at night. You hear a floorboard creak and a door softly opening. Your mind at once suggests what it might be. Maybe something benign: just the wind, or the house re-settling. You wait for another sound. You hear the humming of the fridge, a clock ticking. Lists of alternatives run through your mind. If you feel scared, you imagine the worst. If you feel content and safe (but what is safe?), you might try to return to sleep. Then comes another noise.

Glancing at the clock I saw it was 2.00 a.m. and instantly I knew it was Michael. Before I could even get up out of the bed he was in the room, kneeling down, his forehead resting on the bed at my side. In my mind, I could still see him lying peacefully in his bed, softly snoring.

'I'm sorry, Trish. You made me so angry. I just lost it,' he sobbed.

'How many times do you think I can forgive you, Michael? How long can we go on like this?'

'I know. It won't happen again. I promise.' And yet again, I could see that he really meant it.

I looked straight at him, willing him to look at my split lip, and his eyes obligingly dropped down but quickly rose back to mine again. In all the times he'd hit me, it always surprised me that he could so easily dismiss the result of his rages. Somewhere in the labyrinth of Michael's brain was something that allowed him to forget the pain and damage he'd caused.

'I wanted to talk to you tonight about something but you didn't give me a chance. I saw a take-away business for sale that would be perfect for us. You know how much I hate my job and you're always saying that your part-time job doesn't bring in enough. You could use the extra money. Why don't we buy the business together? We could do it. We both know how to run this sort of business. We'd be great at it. It would make the difference in our relationship that we need. Aren't we worth that chance, Trish? I could even help you with the renovation work around the house that you want to do. What do you say?'

It was true; I hated the thirty-five minute drive to work every day. I hated the rush there for only five hours a day then the rush back to pick up the kids from school at three o'clock. And it was also true that we *could* run a business together. We both had the experience from Pizza Hut.

And God only knew that my house needed renovation. After my divorce, I'd bought this house with a half acre of land for the kids to play in. It had been labelled by the real estate agent as a 'renovator's dream' with a 'babbling brook' cutting the property in half. Very imaginative of the agent because it was actually a fifty-year-old house that was sadly in need of work, with a storm-water drain running through the middle of the property. There was even a toilet pedestal in the front yard, with an asparagus fern growing out of it, that the agent called 'art nouveau'.

But the house was going cheap and I was desperate to find somewhere that the boys could happily call home. I'd imagined them kicking their soccer ball in the large front yard, playing basketball in the back, after I had a landscaper pave the area and put in a hoop for them. Even a dog loping around after them. All dreams, but not improbable ones, even though all I'd managed to do so far was put in the basketball hoop.

Then reality set in. Finding the time to do all of these renovations, not to mention the cash, became my problem. I regarded all quotes from tradesmen as outlandish and I immediately dismissed them. Why couldn't I just do it all myself?

Perhaps you've got this mental vision of a robust woman wielding a hammer and a saw as if born to it. Not the case. My determination was the only tool I had and my skills at carpentry were non-existent. Some boards on the veranda wanted replacing. The interior and exterior of the house needed painting. I'd already pulled up the carpet, revealing firstly Masonite then beautiful wooden floors which needed to be totally sanded back and varnished. I'd done the interior painting by getting up at five o'clock every morning for months and painting until the boys rose at seven. But the exterior was another matter. I'd have to hire someone to do that. Eventually, money becomes the problem, which is why husbands with handymen skills are invaluable. And this was a breed of man I didn't have.

I'm sure he saw my hesitation as a good sign because his look was hopeful even though tentative. 'It'll be good for us. We'll have something to work towards together. The business will be ours to run as we want to, not as someone else says we should. I could move in with you and we'd be a family.'

There you have it. The magic word. Family. And he knew it. He always went for the jugular, always went for my weak spot.

'It'll be perfect. You'll see,' he concluded, smiling his lop-sided smile at me.

And that was how easy it was to slip back into the

black hole. The trap had snapped shut. I forgot the fear I felt as I waited to see what mood he was in when he walked in the door. I forgot about the pain as his fist connected with my mouth. I forgot the cruel words and dreadful names he called me. There is a popular misconception that being hit is worse than being shouted at. They say that words can't hurt but I beg to differ. Long after the bruises have healed, the words still remain to haunt and damage you. My view is that there is no hierarchy of pain. Different women are affected in different ways. Being a punching bag and experiencing psychological abuse in the form of humiliation are almost on a par as far as women are concerned. And he didn't have to work too hard to demean me. I already had a predisposition for being a victim.

But I forgot all of that. What it all boiled down to was I still needed to be loved and wanted. You see, even at this late stage, I was seizing on anything positive, however minor, to make myself more secure in a relationship. I wasn't even sure what a healthy relationship was anymore. I'd segregated myself from human contact and let him win so often that, now, I was thoroughly tired and confused and unable to make a simple decision by myself. Thinking clearly in the midst of fear and chaos is never easy.

I know, I should have said no. I should have, but...
And I should have learnt my lesson, right? Wrong!
That's what should have happened. How could
I possibly have had such low esteem for myself, you
ask? Unfortunately, a lot of women do.

Sadly, it seems that we have to come damn close to
dying, before we come to our senses. It seems that
even when we've been wronged before, even when
we've been fooled by our heart as we've been so
spectacularly fooled before, we stupidly believe that,
at least this time, our brain is working properly.

And so he moved in and we bought the business.

I managed to avoid the expected friction when he
moved in and started removing my possessions and
replacing them with his. Except when it came to putting up his posters of naked and semi-naked women
where the boys could see them. That I wouldn't
allow.

'They're only seven and ten years old,' I reasoned.
I didn't want to get into an argument so early into
the new arrangement but, on this point, I was
adamant. 'You can't put them up in the hallway for
them to see every day.'

I could see the warning signs appearing already. The

pinched mouth. The tic in his eye. All familiar and recognisable. But I couldn't give in on this, could I?

So I made a joke about it. 'No nudes are good nudes.'

Funny, don't you think? Well, I thought so. Michael didn't. While I smiled what I thought was my disarming smile, I watched him clench and unclench his fists. So I compromised.

'If you like them that much, put them up in our bedroom.'

Terrific. Now they'd be the last thing I saw at night and the first thing I saw every morning. But the compromise worked. That's where they went.

The purchase of the shop went smoothly. The previous owners had worked between 8.00 a.m. and 8.00 p.m. but, because it wasn't ideal for my children, Michael and I reached another compromise. I would take the boys to school in the morning then go straight to the shop and open. At 2.00 p.m. he would come in and I would leave at 3.00 p.m. to pick up the boys from school, do the banking and any grocery shopping needed. He would have casual staff to work with him at night. Weekends were a different matter. After taking the boys home on Friday nights, I made them dinner, dropped them off at their basketball games and went back to work at 5.30 p.m., ready for a busy night. By 8.30 p.m. I would be running out the shop's back door to pick up the boys at their club. Then Michael would have Saturdays off while I worked and I had Sundays off while he worked. Not ideal for a fresh start in a floundering relationship but there was no other solution. At least, I reasoned, I could give up golf with a more legitimate excuse than I simply hated it. And don't forget we'd have the nights together.

Even as I say this, I find myself cringing because the nights soon became the worst time of all and it wasn't very long before I realised I'd made yet another disastrous mistake, one you'd probably say should have been obvious. But you see, I truly believed, still do, that out of everything bad comes something good and even if you can't see what it is at the time, sooner or later, all will be revealed. Now, looking back, for the life of me I have no idea what good came out of my 'Michael ordeal'.

What had started out as a business venture soon became a different sort of nightmare. When will she ever learn, you ask? Well, I was asking myself the same question.

In the beginning, he was in a good mood, chatty, and my play acting became easy. Within one month, nothing the employees or I did was good enough. Every night, he'd walk in complaining bitterly about the girls I'd hired. They never cleaned properly, they weren't fast enough, or they were just plain stupid. And it was left up to me to fix the problem. Fire them or train them properly.

The shop actually scared me because it was so busy. At Pizza Hut you did your work and, at the end of a week, you got paid whether it had been a good week or a bad week. Now it was my responsibility to make every week a good one.

Vary the menu, Michael said. At least, *try* to make the food look attractive. And make myself presentable while I was at it. Put tables, chairs and umbrellas outside the shop during the day. Redo the menu boards. Didn't I have any imagination? All this during the daytime hours when I had very little spare time anyway because of the amount of preparation I had to do for the coming nights.

It was my lack of belief in myself that made me blindly go along with what he said. Meanwhile, he arrived at work later and later until he began regularly to arrive at 3.00 p.m. when all I had time to do was run out the door to pick up the boys from school. Then he'd close the shop at 8.00 p.m. every night—which meant he'd only worked five hours during the day when I'd worked seven during the week, ten on Fridays and twelve on Saturdays.

Most days I felt brainwashed, confused, weak, ineffectual and depressed. Depressed most of all. But I was getting tired of the put-downs and intimidation as well, and my Irish spirit surfaced now and then, recklessly it seemed, because it was like waving a red flag in front of a mad bull. Even though I anticipated the possible violent reaction to my rebelliousness, I felt justified. After all, I was entitled to my own opinion, wasn't I?

Then, the fateful night came and everything changed. Our work routine had been in place for a year and the previous night had ended in another terrible row about something inconsequential at the shop. I remember it was a Friday night and I'd already picked up the boys from basketball. It was the Queen's Birthday long weekend and, in the morning, I was going to drop the boys off at their father's house for the three days.

Still lying on the loungeroom floor from the night before were books that had fallen off shelves when Michael had shoved me against the wall hard enough to send them showering down on top of my head. Amongst them, half buried, was a scuffed green plastic binder about six inches long and four inches wide. As it turned out, it was a photo album, the kind with transparent sleeves to hold the photographs in place. Michael had never showed me any pictures of his past life, barely even spoke about it, so to say I was curious is a bit of an understatement. I knew I'd probably never get another chance to look through it, so I took advantage of the situation while the boys showered and got ready for bed.

The first few photos were of two little boys around the ages of four and six. Cute little boys with their arms wrapped around each other. I knew they were of Michael and his brother, Thomas. As the photos progressed, the boys got older until they were in their teens. Still smiling and happy, still standing with their arms casually flung over each other's shoulders.

This couldn't be possible! Thomas was in a wheelchair! Michael had told me so himself on the night of the 'revelation'. I quickly rifled through more photos. There were photos of Thomas obviously at his own wedding, standing with his arms around a smiling bride. Christmas photos of a family with Thomas and Michael standing behind an elderly couple I assumed were their parents. Dozens of photos. All with Thomas standing straight and tall.

Questions and accusations came easily, but not the answers. And, for sure, when I confronted Michael with the evidence, he would be angry with me for snooping through his things. If I was certain of anything about him, it was that.

Whenever I'd asked innocent questions about his childhood, he'd told me bits of stories that seemed a little inconsistent with previous ones. Every day I'd encountered these inconsistencies, the kind that were easily dismissed as misunderstandings on my part or over-simplifications on his.

But now I knew he'd lied to me. No doubt about it. And he had from the very beginning, which is really nothing more than I'd come to expect from him. What he'd actually achieved was nothing more than a sure-footed manoeuvre full of lies and illusions. But illusion, like elastic, does have its breaking points.

Michael, I knew, wasn't a man out of control. He was the opposite. He was a man at work on his own agenda, which was to intimidate and train me to *do* what he wanted and to *be* what he wanted. All the time, controlling, intimidating, manipulating. Like a Chinese water torture. The continual dripping tap that eventually sends you mad. In fact, he was just a weak man who needed to demean and hurt a woman, weaker in physical strength, in order to make himself feel good. He needed me scared and brow-beaten so I would take over all of the daily stresses and occurrences of life to leave him free of any irritation and responsibility.

How on earth had I gotten myself into this, I kept asking? And no, I couldn't blame my resolution to be more trusting. That excuse wouldn't work any more. I'd been fooling myself for too long now. What I'd been doing was trailing around after a maniac making excuses for his behaviour based on a total and complete lie. But I was looking at him through different eyes now. No longer would he fool me into forgiving him. No longer would the desolation in his eyes soften my resolve.

Was I finally going to put an end to it, you ask? You bet I was! About time, you might add. Well, so did I. His influence over me was gone, like an unstable shape formed by smoke that is suddenly blown away by a puff of wind.

This was the catalyst I needed. In the space of the two hours before Michael came home, I began to evaluate and plan. At this point, all I wanted was a way out and I found I had two choices. Stay with him or get him out. There was no way I was going to leave—it was *my* house—so the alternative was to get *him* to leave. Not easy, I know, almost damned impossible, because of the terror that welled up inside of me at the very thought. But it was either become a perpetual victim or remove the cause— which meant removing myself from the partnership in the shop and looking for another job. Well, so be it then! Working on these plans made me feel in control of my own life again, giving me a stronger sense of self. I wouldn't give in this time. I *wouldn't*. I could even visualise my new life. My children, happy and carefree again, not skittering out of the room like frightened crabs whenever Michael walked in. Socialising with friends again. Even just the pleasure of smiling once more. I'd been brain-washed and conditioned to think that I was of no value to anyone but, by God, that was going to end! He'd damaged my self-image and esteem but not irrevocably.

'Start with small steps and the sense of achievement is rewarding enough to move onto the more difficult steps,' I'd heard someone say. That meant removing Michael from my life as the initial step.

So I confronted Michael when he came home that night, after I'd dropped the boys off at their father's house. As I look back now I realise that I must have expected the worst if I'd thought to take the boys out of the house that night instead of the following day. I remember the turmoil of emotions flooding through me and the terror at what he would do when I told him I no longer wanted to be a part of his life. A momentous decision if only I could manage it.

He walked in, dumped the cash register on the table and was in the process of taking the cap off a can of beer when I spoke to him, in as firm a voice as I could. I remember noticing that he was wearing his baggy shorts with a loose polo shirt and his face and arms looked oily with sweat.

'Michael, I want you to buy me out of the business. It's just not working out. I've tried but it's too much for me.'

There, I'd said it. I didn't even bother to mention the photo album. I just stared at his flat empty face. I didn't want to hear any excuses; I couldn't believe a word he said anyway. I didn't want to hear any more statements about how I'd misconstrued what he'd said that night. I didn't want to hear how stupid I was for putting too much emphasis on something that had happened a long time ago. And to tell the truth, I didn't care. I just wanted out.

He raised the can to his mouth and watched me over the bottom of it while he drank, staring with a cold appraising gaze. Cats, both wild and domestic, watch their prey with unblinking regard, alert for the smallest variation in posture, the minutest shift of attention, ready to jump at any sign of weakness. He had that intensity.

Holding tight to my composure, I watched him with equal care. His narrowing eyes, his thick dark hair, his compressed mouth, that tic of his. There was no other emotion. No other reaction. Until he lifted his half-finished can and threw it at my face. When I turned away, he grabbed my hair and yanked me back.

'If you think you're going to ruin me, you've got another think coming. I'll buy you out only because I don't need you. You are nothing. Do you hear? NOTHING!'

It's amazing how fear had become a habit I was learning to live with. I had my eyes closed but I could sense him, smell him, standing over me. Then I opened my eyes. As if in slow motion, I saw his fist rise, then I felt the usual pain as it connected with my face, splitting my lips yet again.

Michael just walked away.

As I slumped to the floor quietly sobbing, I felt the usual sinking inevitability but, this time, something had changed. I thought of all the times he'd done this to me and all the times I'd excused him and forgiven him. I remembered all the vile names he'd called me and almost had me believe. But not anymore. The straw had finally broken the camel's back.

The thought leapt into my head that enough was enough and a surge of adrenalin energised me. Shakily I stood up, licking my lips and tasting blood, and reached out a hand to brace myself against the wall. I would go somewhere tonight. I'd go to another friend of mine I hadn't seen in a while. Linda.

Linda was one of the friends I'd alienated lately simply because Michael didn't want me seeing her without him present and she wouldn't come to my house while he was there. Stalemate. Whenever she saw him, she looked as though she was riding in an aeroplane and it had hit an air pocket.

I picked up my handbag. If I could get out of the house I'd be all right. If I could get to Linda's, I'd be fine. Nearly every week, it seems, I read at least one news story of a man, often estranged from his wife or girlfriend, who kills her then kills himself. Not, I believe, because he fears them or is miserable but as the ultimate act of revenge, punishing those they imagine are beyond their control. *That* was not going to be me.

I remembered stories told to me in my childhood about the bogeyman. There was no such thing, I'd been told, and so he can't get you. But I knew better. Experience had taught me that the bogeyman *did* exist and he could get you at any time. He was not afraid of anything and he didn't respect boundaries.

I felt like I was trying to run while my legs were stuck in thick mud, dragging me down. Panic rushed through me. Against him, I had no chance at all. I stumbled, staggered, gasped and cried and I ran as quietly and quickly as I could to my car. I slowed momentarily as I glanced apprehensively behind me to see if he was coming: but I was safe.

Relieved, I picked up my pace again, seeing my car not twenty feet away. In seconds, I'd be there. Ten feet. Five.

I struggled to open the car door, and then got in quickly, at the same time pressing down the knob to lock the car door. I sat panting, half sobbing, trying to fight down the nausea in my stomach. For several horrible moments, with trembling hands, I fumbled for the ignition key and tried to fit it into the tiny lock. I was in no fit state to drive—but that was the last thing that I was thinking about. I don't believe I was thinking at all.

I stopped at a pay phone on the way to Linda's house, my head still spinning; first, to see if she was home and, second, to tell her what had happened.

Chapter 9

Escape to Linda's House

Driving away from my house that night was not as liberating as I'd hoped it would be. All it did was make me realise that this was only a temporary escape and that my life was like a huge bubble; rather than breaking free of it, I was simply stretching it around me to include others. I burst abruptly into tears, great surging lumps of emotion which almost choked me. My stomach churned and my head throbbed.

Linda's house, number 5, was set back from the road and I had to drive down a winding easement before pulling up at her front door. The veranda light was on and, in the semi-darkness, I could see the heavy branches of a grevillea covering her loungeroom window, reducing the light from inside to a shifting glitter.

When I walked into Linda's house, the ceiling light was on and, as I turned away from the front door, she just stared at me. Tonight, her hair was auburn; last month it had been light blonde, the month before caramel. You never knew what hair colour would greet you from one day to the next.

'You look fantastic,' she said sarcastically. 'You didn't tell me that your face was in this kind of a state.'

I almost laughed. This kind of a state? Christ, this was good compared to what it had been on some occasions. Still, I must have looked a sight. I could feel the shiny smoothness of the swelling on my lips and taste the blood again in my mouth.

I walked over to her and put my arms around her.

'Just hold me,' was all I said.

I couldn't help noticing that she had on a lovely little black number with high-heeled shoes and smelled softly of Opium.

'I'm sorry,' I said, pulling gently away from her, 'you're on your way out.' I felt like apologising for my own appearance; jeans again and a blue singlet top that had shrunk in the last wash and now showed my belly-button.

'Come and have a drink. I'm not going anywhere now. And don't start apologising again,' she said when she saw me open my mouth. 'You've got to get out of that habit.'

Either it was too warm in the house or she'd already had a couple of drinks before I'd arrived because her cheeks were flushed and her eyes were shining. Her next words told me there was anger as well.

'I hope *this time* you get rid of that scum.' She fairly

spat the words out as she led me through an arch into the kitchen.

Linda swore, smoked heavily and drank too much but she was the most honest, reliable person I knew and although she had a lot of good qualities, tact wasn't one of them. She always spoke her mind and, if she didn't like a person, she said so in no uncertain terms. Which is why Michael hated her. She once told him that the doctor should have thrown him out and kept the afterbirth.

'Did you manage to get out with an overnight bag?' she asked over her shoulder.

I shook my head.

'Fantastic,' she said again, only softer this time, her tone full of scorn now, instead of anger.

She reached in the fridge for an already-opened bottle of white wine, Chardonnay I think it was, and filled the two glasses that were sitting on the kitchen bench.

She handed one glass to me and then turned, carrying the bottle with her, and walked back into the loungeroom again, speaking as she went. 'I hope you don't mind me asking, but what the hell are you going to do now?'

I leaned against the arch as she plonked herself in a leather two-seater.

'Please Linda,' I said wearily. 'Not tonight. I know I have to do something. I'm just not sure what that is yet.'

She looked at me over the top of her glass, sipping the dry wine. Slowly she lowered the glass and patted the seat next to her with the other hand. 'Come and sit down.'

All anger had gone out of her voice and I could hear the pity in it now. That was enough to start the tears rising to the surface again.

I put the glass down on a side table and did as I was told, just like I'd been doing for the past many months, and hugged myself while I tried not to cry yet again.

'I can't believe you're the same person I met five years ago,' she said softly as she refilled her glass. We'd met when we'd both been waitresses at Pizza Hut. She went on to do office work full time while I'd gone on to do a manager's training course. We'd kept in touch over the years but recently we hadn't seen each other much at all, thanks to Michael.

Even as I say that, I realise it wasn't all Michael's fault. It was as much my fault for allowing it to happen, allowing him to rule my life and take over so completely that any thought or decision had to be run by him first.

'When I saw you outside on the veranda tonight, your face was like a little girl's; you looked scared and alone and like that bloody orphanage had just slammed its door in your face.'

At once, I felt a lump in my throat and, to my surprise, found myself sobbing. I put my hands to my face to cover the tears and felt Linda's hand stroking my hair.

'Come on. You'll be fine. We'll sort this out. Pick up your glass and drink your wine.'

I sniffed, running the back of my hand under my nose, and calmed myself, sniffing again.

'I've been trying to work out what you should do,' she said. 'It's not easy. After I've been through the options, stabbing him always seems the best solution.'

I smiled as she gazed at me thoughtfully. For a moment I thought she was going to come up with some startling insight, produce some wonderful plan that I'd overlooked. Instead she said, 'What I keep coming back to is that for you to get your self-confidence and self-esteem back, you've got to do this for yourself. No-one can do it for you. You've got to want your life back so bad that you'll do anything to get it.'

She held up her hand when she saw the hurt and surprise on my face. 'I didn't say I wouldn't help, but all I can do is support you and be there for you whenever you need me. *You* have to be the one to put a stop to it. *You* have to be the one to tell him to get out and stay out. I can't do that for you. It's not my decision. It's yours.'

Despite drinking the wine on an empty stomach, making my head swim, I could tell it was hard for her to say all this. Her forehead was puckered into a frown and her mouth was turned down at the sides as she shook her head.

'Can I make myself a cup of coffee?' I asked.

'Go ahead.'

'You want one too?'

She held up her half-empty glass and said, 'And waste this? What planet are you from?'

I walked into the kitchen and, as I did, the motion detector light came on in the backyard, making me jump. As I stood framed in the window, I imagined seeing Michael fly into view on the other side of the window, his face twisted in rage.

Deep inside, I knew it couldn't be him; it was only the wind blowing the trees around or some cat walking through the yard, but even still, my heart was doing somersaults inside my chest.

He has no idea I'm here, I told myself. I doubted he would come even if he *did* know; he hated Linda so much.

I felt vulnerable standing there in the brightly lit unfamiliar kitchen and it took me a good ten minutes to make the coffee. While I waited for the kettle to boil, I thought about what Linda had said.

She was right and I knew it. Did I really want to spend the rest of my life, hiding my thoughts and feelings behind the threat of Michael's fist? Hadn't my early years in the orphanage and foster homes taught me anything at all? Was I going to jump in panic at sudden noises and lights forever?

As I stared out of the window, I wondered where was the fire that I used to feel in my youth. Where was the determination that no-one, no-one, was ever going to turn me into a victim again?

It had been temporarily bullied out of me but the embers of that fire were still smouldering beneath the surface, waiting to be rekindled. It was up *me* to put an end to the pain and heartache and make a stand. No-one else could do it for me. Enough was enough. And I *would* do it. I *would*.

I walked back into the room and Linda smiled up at me lazily. I noticed the bottle was now empty and the glass she was holding had barely a mouthful left in it. 'I think I'm a bit pissed. I had a few drinks before you arrived.'

'You've helped me tonight more than you know.'

She put her glass down on the floor beside her chair and stood up. 'It's all about seeing and not seeing.'

'What do you mean?'

She opened her mouth to speak but giggled instead. 'Haven't the faintest idea. I'm rather drunk. I don't know what I'm talking about.'

She hiccupped and put her hand over her mouth, swaying a little uncertainly on her feet. As she did, she tipped over her almost empty wine glass with the toe of her shoe. 'Whoops,' she said. 'Alcohol abuse.'

We looked at each other and giggled. She leant down and picked up the glass and wafted her hand in the direction of the bedrooms. 'My room's on the right. You can have your choice of the other two.'

She put the glass on the table and walked out with as much dignity as she could, given she'd had far too much to drink and was wearing four-inch heels.

'G'night,' she said as she disappeared into her bedroom.

The next day was Saturday and Michael called me at the shop, irritated that he'd woken up alone, calling me childish.

'You've hit me for the last time,' I told him.

'It was just an argument. Why make more out of it than it was? Why exaggerate it out of all proportion? You always do that.'

Once upon a time, I wouldn't have had the courage to argue but I didn't care anymore. Emboldened by my decision of the previous night and running my tongue over my swollen lip, I said, 'It's over Michael. I want you to either buy my share of the shop or we sell it. I don't want to see you again. I want you out of my life, out of my house this afternoon and I want my key back.'

'I'm not going to talk to you while you're in this mood,' he argued.

'I don't want to talk to you ever again,' I countered.

'Fine. Let's not,' and before I could repeat that I wanted my key back, he'd put the phone down.

Despite his words, during the day he kept calling back, gradually getting more and more contrite while I tried explaining that I'd had enough.

Finally, I guess the realisation hit him when I asked him to be gone from the house that afternoon, leaving the key behind, and to come and collect the rest of his things on the weekend when a friend of mine would be with me. Not before.

He turned to wheedling and said, 'I've changed, Trish. I know I had a problem but I've sorted all that out.'

Beneath his quiet manner, I could sense something not quite right. Like a painting sitting askew on a wall. I wonder now why I didn't see all of these things before.

'Michael, it's over. You've hit me more times than I care to remember but now it's over. You're not going to control me anymore. I am my own person.' I can remember saying those exact words and thinking it sounded like an emotional response, something I didn't want it to be.

'Haven't you been listening to me?' His voice was sharp and I braced myself for the inevitable. 'I said I was bloody sorry.'

Up until then, I'd thought our relationship had a chance of ending rationally. How many times had he promised to change? Deep inside I knew that, despite his pledge, the abuse would never stop. There would always be a temporary respite to regain trust but eventually the pattern would resume. Now, I took a deep breath and repeated, 'You've hurt me too many times.'

I felt so brave saying those simple words. Free from the hold he had over me.

'But I mean it this time.'

'And you didn't mean it before?'

'Don't get smart with me, Trish. Give me a chance to explain.'

I touched my lip again with my tongue. It still tasted raw. I sighed. To get him off the phone, I agreed to meet him at 3.30 p.m. during my break but I had no intention of doing that at all.

Two o'clock came, and I rang him back, telling him

I couldn't make it. I made up the excuse that I had to see Sue during my break and I'd be unable to meet him after all. Again, I told him that it wouldn't make any difference; I still wanted him to leave that afternoon then come and pick up his things on the weekend.

I ended by hanging up the phone while he was still telling me how much he'd changed.

Chapter 10

A Trapped Animal

I knew who it was without even looking. I knew the sound of the tyres on the concrete. The drone of his car's engine. Everything.

I was terrified, doing my best to breathe. When I swallowed my throat hurt. I thought I heard heavy footsteps on the planks of the stairs.

Everything inside of me contracted. My heart was pounding and my insides felt like water. I was shaking so much I could feel my limbs trembling as if from cold. I couldn't move. I just stood there staring at the door, barely breathing so as not to make a noise, while I waited for it to open.

Then a figure materialised outside the window. Bulky and shapeless. It stood there for a few seconds. I heard a key in the lock before I saw the door knob move and the door open. As the figure stood in the doorway, my eyes tried desperately to adjust to the sudden light. It surrounded him like a halo making his body a silhouette. The shape came slowly and quietly. First the chest, then the body and then the head until the doorway was filled. In that uncertain light, the hand on the doorknob looked monstrous.

I pressed the back of one of my shaking hands to my mouth to stop an involuntary gasp from escaping and I leaned, cold and sick, against the kitchen bench. The light he'd been blocking blurred and shifted and I saw Michael's face in the dim light.

Of course it was Michael! Who else had I thought it would be? In my mind I was hoping for someone else. An escapee from a prison, a burglar, a serial killer on the loose but, please God, not Michael.

I didn't move. I couldn't. My body felt cool from the cold shower I'd had and my hair was still wet but I felt like I had a temperature or a fever making me sweat. My eyes blinked uncontrollably and I looked around me for an escape, somewhere to run. When I looked at Michael again, when my heart had stopped beating so fast, his eyes were all screwed up as he smiled sardonically at me.

'Waiting for a bus, are we?'

When he spoke, terror swam inside me as though a hand had grabbed my heart. My chest began to pound again and I thought I was going to faint. Innocent enough words, 'waiting for a bus,' but I knew what was coming. I could see it in his eyes. Those black eyes that seemed to glisten darkly in the luminous whiteness surrounding them.

I managed to shake my head stupidly.

He smiled. Not a nice smile. Forced. Stretching his lips to expose his teeth. There was something in his expression that made me sharply conscious of the situation I was in: deeply in. I was alone. Any help I got now would come only from myself and I was well aware that I am not the stuff of which heroines are made.

'I'm... I'm expecting someone. You'd...ah...you can't stay,' I lied.

I'm not a good liar. I blush and stutter and look everywhere but at the face of the person I'm talking to. He knew it was a lie straightaway.

'Ah,' he said. 'The Cavalry comes.'

He stood looking at me like a teacher who'd caught me doing something I shouldn't and was trying to decide how I should be punished. I saw his jawbone flex.

'You have to go,' I repeated, my voice cracking. 'The boys will be home soon.' Another lie. The boys were with their father and he knew it.

'Not yet.' He took a step towards me and involuntarily, I took one backwards.

'Do you know why I'm here?' His eyes stared at me, not blinking, his voice soft and intense. Measured.

'No,' I said as I shook my head. My voice was so quiet; I could hardly even hear it.

'First, I want you to tell me who else you've been seeing besides me,' he asked.

I blinked and managed to say, 'What?' shook my head vehemently and gasped. Was this what his visit was all about? Jealousy over an imagined lover? Momentarily, relief flooded me because I wasn't guilty of any such offence.

'Michael, no! Think about it. When would I have found the time? You knew where I was at every minute of the day.' Past tense. Knew. Was.

Being reasonable is something I've learnt from my time with Michael. Explaining things in detail as if reasoning with a child: most of the time to no avail.

I started to walk away. The atmosphere had changed in the room suddenly, from menace to outright anger. Was it my own long-suspended anger that filled the room?

Michael's response was immediate, as if I'd flicked a switch.

'Where do you think you're going?' he said as he grabbed my shoulder and shoved me back against the breakfast bench. He was trying not to sound angry, speaking through gritted teeth as if *I* was the one doing something wrong. Moisture had formed in his eyes and, for a moment, I thought he was going to cry.

I pushed myself off the bench, about to talk, when he began speaking again.

'I spoke to Sue this afternoon after you rang to say you couldn't see me. You remember Sue, don't you? Sue's the friend you *had* to see today instead of coming to see me. But guess what? Sue knew nothing about it. Surprise, surprise!'

He regarded me through eyes as small as slits. 'Why lie, Trisha, if you weren't doing anything wrong? See? I *don't* know where you are at every minute of the day, do I? So tell me, Trish, where the f... were you this afternoon?'

His voice was so soft it belied the words he'd spoken. He was so close now, I could smell the pungent combination of sweat and aftershave.

By then, I'd resigned myself to the fact that soon the horrible pain would begin again. Even as I thought those words, I saw Michael ball his right hand into a fist and I waited for it to connect again with my face.

When Michael flew into a rage he would use anything close at hand as a weapon. A book, my handbag, the kettle. Self-restraint was always a tortuous struggle for Michael. He once hit me continuously with a rolled-up newspaper until it fell apart in tatters on the floor. He once threw a tomato at me, which might sound funny but it wasn't at the time. It hit my mouth and split my lip making it difficult for me to eat for days afterwards. Nothing he did left disfiguring scars, but the emotional ones are there. They're what's left after eighteen months of fear and pain; from when we began by smiling and we ended up—*I* ended up—terrified for my life.

'ANSWER ME!' he screamed in my face.

Curry, I thought. He's had curry for lunch. It's funny the things that register when the unbelievable is happening. I could see veins beginning to pop out on his forehead and, if I'd wanted to, I could have traced with my finger a swollen one that led from an eyebrow into his hair.

'Shopping,' I said in an almost steady voice.

A sneer spread across his face. 'Guess what else Sue said?' He stared at me deadpan. 'Huh?'

I shrugged.

'Lewis's having an affair.'

At first, his statement didn't register. This was old news to me. Sue had suspected Lewis of having an affair for months now but she had no proof of anything.

'So I've heard,' I replied.

'Guess what else she said?'

I waited while he regarded me coolly. Did he want me to answer? I looked down at his hands, bracing myself for the attack. His hands were big with long fingers with thick knuckles. I didn't know how much I'd come to hate those hands.

I shrugged nonchalantly, trying to hide my fear of him, not wanting to give him the satisfaction of knowing that he scared the life out of me.

'Sue doesn't know where Lewis was this afternoon either.'

Only then did I know where things were headed.

I felt my eyes widening in shock. I could feel myself becoming hysterical with fear. Tears were welling at the back of my eyes now and as much as I tried not to, I knew I was going to cry.

'Whores like you don't deserve men like me. They need to be punished.'

A cold terrible fear sliced through me because I could see he meant it.

'Don't do this Michael,' I whispered. My head was shaking of its own volition. I saw his eyes bulging and I remember cringing, sure a physical assault was going to replace the verbal one.

I felt his fist before I saw it. It went straight into my chest with a crunch. Tears were running down my cheeks by then as I lowered my head. Drawing in a breath, I placed a hand over my chest between my breasts. He hit me again, this time on my mouth, and I was propelled backwards, too quickly for my legs to cope, my arms flung out wide to balance myself.

I landed on my rump, pain shooting up my back and into my head. The taste of blood filled my mouth once more and, with my tongue, I gingerly felt the reopened cut on my lip where my teeth had gone through. There was an enormous buzzing going on in my brain and millions of stars crossed my vision. I raised my hands to my face and they came away wet with tears and blood.

Everything had seemed in slow motion, almost unreal; only the sickness in my stomach and the pain in my chest were real. I was surprised at how much I hurt inside, as if I was made of glass and pieces of me kept shattering and falling away so that no-one could put me back together.

Michael towered over me, shouting in my face and I realised that the bees in my head were so loud, they drowned out his words and I remember thinking that's just as well. I could see his mouth moving quite clearly but I couldn't hear what he was saying. Then he turned and walked away.

My mind took one of those wrong turns and I began to rationalise.

I know. This is a dream. I'll wake up and I'll be in bed alone, Michael won't be here and everything will be fine. Then I almost smiled. I felt the sharp pain in my lip and knew this wasn't a dream and Michael wasn't a ghost. Ghosts don't eat curry and they can't split your lip.

I could feel the tears coming again but I tried to fight them back. Funny thing. I'd never been a crier. I'd always kept my defiant and 'who cares' face showing even if I was screaming inside. I'd made myself numb because I believed tears are nonsense.

But since meeting Michael, it was like I'd thrown the door open and let the pain in. And it hurt. Where had I gone wrong? This was supposed to be *my* time for finding myself and getting a fresh start. But again, I'd screwed up.

I don't know how long I sat there. You lose track of time. It felt like half-an-hour but was probably no more than five minutes. I tried to breathe and stay calm. Be rational. Maybe I should just pack up my kids and run. Lock up the house and put it in the hands of a real estate agent. Run away and change my name.

I'd once played a game when I was young because my name was so strange. Patricia Gourgaud. Gourgaud. The way to pronounce it, it sounds like something a baby says. Goo ga. So I'd played my game. Take my middle name, Therese, and make it my first name. Then use the name of the street where I was living as my surname. During my five years of fostering, I'd had a choice of about twenty different names.

They say it takes a while to comprehend a tragedy. You can't accept the reality. I don't think that's true. Not for me anyway. I understood the full implications the moment I went to my first foster home. I understood I'd never be going back to my parents. I understood it was final and that there'd be no reprieve. No negotiation or bargaining. Changing my name had been the way of dealing with my anger and hurt at being so easily disposed of.

Every muscle in my body felt weak and as the minutes ticked by, the terrible reality of what had happened pressed itself on me. At first my mind refused to accept the truth, still clinging to the last vestige of hope that I was mistaken about the extent of Michael's cruelty. But as I sat on the floor, I couldn't deny it anymore.

I stood up slowly and began hobbling towards my bedroom gasping for breath, my mind fogged with pain. It's strange the things you remember when pain is the only sensation you feel. Pictures on the walls, a mirror where I saw a scarecrow looking back at me. A large dust bunny in a corner of the dining-room. I passed a bookcase where some books had fallen and were now lying horizontally across the vertical ones. All I wanted to do was reach my bed-room, or more specifically, the bed.

On the bedside table was a lamp, a clock and a packet of Panadol beside a glass of water. I took out two tablets and swallowed them with some of the water, leaving a smear of blood on the rim of the glass. As I lay down, I vowed that this would never happen to me again. *You are of no importance to me, Michael. You are gone.*

To say I felt sick, scared, vulnerable and totally alone is probably an understatement. I curled up into a foetal position and wrapped my arms around my body and cried.

Eventually, I opened my eyes and caught the remains of a fading shadow. So fragile. Like the shadowy pattern of leaves on the lawn. I almost whispered 'Dad?' but stopped myself. The street light caught and elongated the shadow for a moment. *Maybe Michael is right. Maybe I am unbalanced,* I thought. *If I am mad, there is a wonderful liberation in my madness.*

I wanted to do what I did when I was a child. I used to travel many miles in my mind. To the great rolling ocean full of power and strength, rising and heaving. Then suddenly, for some reason, the ability to do it left me.

I lay sleepless and tried to make myself relax, tried to uncurl my body and breathe slowly. I noticed that I'd crossed my arms over my chest as though it was the most natural thing in the world to do, the way Sister Philomena used to say protected you from evil. My hands were clenched and even my legs were crossed. It was a typical defensive pose, I suppose. Bracing myself against another attack and making myself as small a target as I could. I might be a victim but I hated looking like one, retreating like a turtle inside my shell. At one time, I became aware that my hands actually hurt because I'd been clenching them tightly into fists for so long.

I tried to lay still and let all the negative energy flow out of me. That's when I knew something terrible was there in the darkness. Something nearby. I could hear my heart beating abnormally fast. So fast it reminded me of a tiny sparrow I'd held not so long ago that had fallen out of its nest. I'd cupped its soft body in my hands and felt its heart beating so rapidly it seemed like a constant vibration rather than a heartbeat.

Then I felt the bed move as Michael lay down beside me.

In the silence, I could hear his heavy breathing just before the phone rang, making us both jump. He flexed the fingers of his right hand where the bruises on his knuckles were beginning to show and let go of my jumper before he switched the bedside light on and picked up the phone.

'Hello'. His voice was gentle. 'Sue? Great. How are you?'

I closed my eyes to stop the light shining in and sending sharp pain through my skull. *Sue. So close.*

'She's in the bath, Sue. Shall I get her to call you back?... She'd love that... okay. Talk to you soon. Bye.'

His voice was so soft but with the call over, I began to shake.

'That was Sue,' he whispered. 'She wants to know if we can go over to her house for dinner tomorrow night after work.'

So conversational.

'Open your eyes, darling, and look at me when I'm talking to you.'

I managed it.

'There you are. Not so hard is it? I'm not going to hurt you.'

He picked up a pillow and lifted my head gently to position it for my comfort.

He walked around to my side of the bed and knelt down beside me. 'You shouldn't try to make me angry, you know. Should you?' he said looking down at his bruised hand. '*Should you?*' His voice rose.

'No,' I whispered.

'You'll have to tell Sue we can't go.'

Tears were rising in my eyes again and began to trickle out.

'Oh Trish. I never want to hurt you, you know that.

I'll run a bath and then pop you in bed with a nice hot cup of tea.'

I heard him go away and then water running in the bath. He lifted me and stood me by the bath then gently undressed me before helping me into the bath.

The water was beautifully warm and slowly I began to stop shaking.

He sponged me with infinite tenderness and then towel-dried me gently. After helping me to put on my nightie, he walked me back to bed and tucked me in.

'Now for that tea.'

It seemed only a minute later that I felt his hand behind my head as he directed a cup to my split lips and helped me drink through a straw. Then he gave me another two Panadol and stroked my hair as I tried to swallow them.

'I'm so sorry. I never meant to hurt you.'

I leant back and said nothing. *Please go,* I screamed inside my head.

As if reading my mind, he stood up. 'We're not going to talk anymore about leaving me, are we? Are we?'

I shook my head silently.

'You know you can't do without me looking after you. I only pushed you and look what happened. You're so clumsy.' He continued stroking my hair.

I tried not to move. Tried to lie still on my back so that the huge ache that I'd become would fade for a while. For a minute, I wished for death. An oblivion where silence and darkness would swallow me up.

Michael stood up. There was a moment rustling as he put on his dressing-gown and then there was a pause, 'I'll sleep in the loungeroom tonight so that I won't disturb you in the morning when I go to work.' Then the bedroom door closed.

In the silence, I thought of my friends who had slipped and faded away, confused by my distance. I thought of Sue and Linda and then stopped because it would only make me cry and the pain would return again. I remember vaguely hearing the rain outside, and slowly felt myself relaxing, the Panadol working. I was too tired to think anymore, too tired and sore to move. I wanted the world to fade away and let me sink into limbo where nothing hurt. If I lay very still, it didn't hurt as much. Nothing could touch me here. I melted into the darkness and heard my own breathing rising and falling sporadically.

I knew now how people went mad: they gave up fighting. They went mad because it was a hell of a lot easier. They went mad because they went to a far better place. You get tired of the constant battle with no victories and no ceasefires. You lose your grip on the world slowly and drift into the chasm of your own unhappiness and hopelessness. I was suspended above the chasm, hovering unsteadily, feeling my grip slipping. No hope, no relief, no reprieve—ever.

I hate to admit that even suicide entered my head but, of course, my children were always on my mind and I knew that it wasn't an option. How would they ever forgive me? The odd thing is, you can't see the light at the end of the tunnel.

Before I finally dropped off to sleep, I turned towards the phone. It was so tempting to call Sue but it was more than my life was worth.

Chapter 11

I'd Become a Statistic

We take life for granted. Each day we carry on as though nothing will change. We go on with our lives feeling bored or even blasé until that life is irrevocably changed. Then, we realise.

There I was, sitting in a waiting room at the hospital at nine o'clock in the morning amongst a disparate group of cold sufferers, people with injured limbs and frail old ladies. I sat as still as I could, taking tiny puffs of breath to reduce the pain in my chest enough so that I could breathe.

If I'd slept at all the previous night, neither my body nor my mind had benefited from it. My head hurt and my back was sore from lying perfectly still to lessen the pain in my chest. I'd tried to clean my teeth and brush my hair but I knew I'd done a bad job. The lid of my left eye was swollen and no amount of makeup was going to cover it up, or the split lip.

Five hours later, I had the results of the x-rays.

'You've sustained an injury to your sternum,' the doctor said while staring at the picture of my chest on the screen. 'Actually, there's a small break right there.' He pointed to a faint line that I probably wouldn't have seen if he hadn't pointed it out. He spun around on his chair and pursed his lips. 'That's not an easy thing to do.'

I kept taking in tiny puffs of breath as he looked at me. 'You're going to feel wobbly for a while. There's not a lot we can do except prescribe rest.'

I continued puffing.

'Are you going to press charges against him?' he asked.

If I could have laughed, I would have. What good would pressing charges do? Michael knew where I lived and he was dangerous. He'd find some way to pay me back.

Instead of making some inane excuse about falling over, I decided to simply tell the truth. No more excuses about walking into a door. No more tripping episodes or clumsy falls. Just the truth.

'Pressing charges will only make things worse than they already are,' I whispered.

'So he gets away with it. Is that what you're saying?'

He sat back in his leather chair and made a steeple of his fingers while he rested his elbows on the arm-rests. 'Let me ask you a few questions and quote you a few statistics. Did you know that domestic violence is the major cause of injury to women and that, after the first major study of battered women in 1976, it was estimated that one quarter of Australian women experience physical assault; one third in the United States?' He let that sink in.

'It is truly difficult for me and other colleagues of mine to accept the sorry fact that there are a large number of women who actually shackle themselves to controlling and obsessive men. Congratulations, you may now put yourself in the same category as the battered women who make up the twenty per cent of all emergency visits to the hospital by women. As women who are in nine times greater danger of being a victim in their own home than in a motor car. This is like a silent epidemic occurring across all economic, ethnic, cultural and religious groups.'

If these facts are frightening to you, they scared the hell out of me. I never thought I'd become a statistic.

'What is even scarier,' he continued unrelentingly as I began to squirm in my seat, 'is that like rape, the crime of domestic violence is under-reported because it usually occurs at home and with no witnesses. If you do nothing about this, you're actually over-looking and condoning his behaviour. Is this how you want to live? Let him feel that he has gotten away with his crime and that he can perhaps do this to you again or even to another woman? Can you live with that? My suggestion to you is to eliminate the problem. And by the looks of it, you should do it quickly.'

He reached over to a booklet that was sitting on his desk. 'I took the liberty of getting this for you. It's a booklet that identifies the seven steps that help you to get out of this sort of situation.' He handed it to me. 'I'd like you to read it.'

A pretty speech from someone who had never felt the force of Michael's fist splitting his lips, closing his eyes or breaking the bone that holds his ribs together so that every breath is pure agony. He'd never seen the savage look in Michael's eyes or heard the venom with which he spoke when his rage took over.

But even as the doctor finished speaking, I knew he was right. Life was transitory. This day would roll into the next and the next and the next. But only if I let it. It was only then I realised that Michael knew how to play me. He knew to wrap his arms around me and woo me with a voice full of love. The voice he used only for me when he knew he'd gone too far. He would try to wrap me up in his dark blanket of twisted emotion and he would be single-minded in his intensity. But it would soon end and things would go back to the way they always were.

For a time, I wouldn't have to dread seeing his mouth compressed into a tight line or the tic in his left eye. I wouldn't have to feel the anxiety that would start in my stomach. I wouldn't have to rehearse in my mind what I would say before I dared say it. Or try it first to myself in case I provoked a sudden burst of temper.

But it would happen. No matter how many times he told me he was sorry, it would happen. Again… and again… and again. Slowly, bit by bit, he was killing my spirit and, once that died, it would be no surprise when the rest went too.

I tasted the last of the blood in my mouth and looked down at the booklet. The words 'Seven Steps to Freedom' looked back at me.

'Will you write a letter for me, stating the extent of my injuries?'

He smiled broadly. 'It would give me the greatest pleasure. Tomorrow, we'll do that. But tonight, you stay in the hospital.'

Chapter 12

Finally Knowing
What I Had to Do

Waking in a hospital is so different. You know immediately where you are. Before you even open your eyes, you hear the rattle of teacups outside the door and the gentle murmur of traffic in the corridor.

I felt distinctly better than I had the day before, almost lulled into a strange floating amnesia. This is when the doubts set in. *Maybe I over-reacted? Maybe things weren't as bad as I thought?*

'Good morning. How're you feeling?'

A nurse stood by my bed, as if by magic, shaking a thermometer as she smiled down at me. She stuck the thermometer in my mouth avoiding the cut on my lip and I mumbled a reply as she checked my pulse with her fob watch.

She whipped the thermometer out, looked at it, and shook it again. 'That's good,' she said as she wrote the results on a chart at the end of my bed. 'Do you want a painkiller?'

'No. I just ache now.'

'Good girl. I'll be back later when doctor does his rounds. In the meantime, you can try and have some light breakfast, if you want.'

'Just tea,' I managed and she nodded.

I closed my eyes and tried to move onto my side. Tears of pain mixed with self-pity pinched behind my eyes as I listened to my breath puffing in the empty room. The shutters were drawn on the windows and, in the half-light, I heard the swoosh of someone moving around the room.

I opened my eyes to see boots. My eyes travelled upwards and there was a policewoman looking down at me.

'Looks like you made a lucky escape,' she said. 'Your doctor said you were going to press charges. Is that correct?'

I nodded.

'Good,' she said. 'There are some things that you can't sweep under the carpet.'

She turned around and dragged a chair closer to the bed then sat down. 'There's not much I can do from here. What you'll have to do is go down to the station and make a statement and they'll take it from there. It won't be easy but you can't continue on with your life as if nothing has happened. I know because I was in your position once myself.'

'But you're a policewoman.' The idea astounded me that someone in a job such as hers could ever have had the same experiences as I had.

'This sort of thing can happen to anyone. No-one's immune, believe me. I guess you could say I fell headlong into *my* first marriage. I had set ideas of what my marriage was going to be like but within one year, I knew I'd made a dreadful mistake. I really didn't know the man I'd married. One day he was so caring and gentle, or I thought he was, and then, for no reason at all, he'd change. His temper had a short fuse: smiling one minute, look out the next. One night it came to a head and we had this almighty row and he beat me up. I ended up with both my eyes black and a broken arm.

'Of course, he was sorry and said he'd never do it again. What he didn't know at the time was that I was pregnant. It was lucky I managed to keep the baby and for a while I think *that* scared him more than anything else and there were no more episodes for almost two years.

'I wouldn't believe it could ever happen again. I thought that after the last time when I was pregnant, the terrible consequences would make him realise he'd gone too far and he'd be cured of any aggressive outbursts. That lasted for two years. Then, there I was again with a concussion after he chased me down the hall, slamming me up against the bathroom door. All because I tried to stop him from yelling at the baby for crying. I crawled into the bathroom and lay there listening to the thumping on the door and the pitiful sounds of my baby crying. That's when I realised he'd never change and that I couldn't exist like that.

'He slept off his anger and the next day acted as if nothing had happened. It's amazing how scary *that* is. When they don't even care how much they've hurt you. You realise that, if that's how they feel, then they will definitely keep doing it. It's almost worse than listening to the pathetic promises that it would never happen again. The next day when he was at work, I bundled up the baby and packed as many things as I could in my car and left. I stayed with a friend until I got a flat of my own with support from Help Line. Eventually, I got a divorce.'

I could see the similarities between us: the waiting for the inevitable to happen, the perpetual promises and then the realisation that it was all a lie.

'What you've got to realise,' she continued, 'is that if it's been going on for a while now, it's not going to stop and you have to put an end to the relationship. It's a hard road but believe me, there *is* a happy ending. And most of all, you needn't be alone. There are support groups who will help.'

I was silent for a while. She was right. I had to take some action or else my life would just be a misery.

'Okay,' she said as she stood up. 'As soon as you're discharged from the hospital, you go straight down and start proceedings.' She smiled and patted my shoulder. 'You're doing the right thing. You've got to have faith in that. Don't fall into the trap of thinking you're by yourself in this.'

She glanced over at the booklet on my side table and picked it up.

'This is very good. It outlines everything I've been saying. Read it as soon as you can. Okay?' She handed it to me.

I nodded and took it from her.

In the quiet that followed, I sat and listened to the fan blowing air around the room, heard footsteps and the echoes in the hall outside. How many similar decisions had been made by people sitting right where I was now? How many people had stared at the floor, heard the same sounds and prayed to a God they weren't sure either existed or cared.

'There's a gentleman outside to see you.' A nurse had walked in and was standing at the bottom of my bed.

It could only be Michael. For a moment, I thought the world had tilted. There was the sound of the ocean roaring in my ears and I could feel my heart pounding as I imagined him outside, talking and laughing with the nurses. He'd win them over as he smiled at them. Remember, he could sparkle when he wanted to. They'd listen to his quiet voice and watch his almost shy mannerisms. They'd see the Michael he wanted them to see: quietly concerned, distressed at the extent of my injuries, shocked even at my accusations. They wouldn't know how he could change his moods in the space of a minute or that his changes were as calculated as Robert Louis Stevenson's character, Jekyll and Hyde. They wouldn't know that Michael could act like the respectful Jekyll who created the vicious Hyde to act out his fantasies—although in the book, and unlike Michael, Jekyll's power struggle was inside his body and he was always in control.

Then they'd come in here with suspicion in their eyes and see me. Defensive. Distrustful. Wary. Why did I imagine anyone would believe me instead of him? Could I even blame them? I'd been dim-witted enough not to see through his impressive act myself.

I stupidly sat trembling, almost violently shaking my head. No words would come out. Thankfully, I didn't have to say anything.

'Don't worry,' she said softly as she came around to

the side of my bed and patted my hand, 'I'll tell him you aren't up to visitors.'

What I wanted to hear was that there was hope and that I wouldn't have to see him alone ever again. The world would stop tilting and my life would make sense.

I listened to the murmuring from the other side of the door. The quiet rumble of Michael's voice as it gradually began to rise, becoming more adamant and insistent. The soft but firm replies from the nurse. Then the retreating footsteps. And silence. Blessed silence.

I looked down at the booklet in my hand. Now, more than ever, I needed to know that help was close by. The words 'Seven Steps to Freedom'* stared back at me. *Man, if that were only true!* I opened the pamphlet and began reading.

In the next few hours, the nurse came back in and took my temperature again. At that time of day, the hospital would have been bustling with rounds, meals and medication. Tea cups would have been rattling on trolleys down the corridors. The smell of antiseptic would be mingling with toast and coffee.

---

*'The Seven steps to Freedom' are given in detail at the end of this book after Epilogue.

The sound of clanging bedpans and trolleys, plus occasional moans, would greet anyone as they walked through the wards.

I hardly acknowledged anything going on around me. The pamphlet totally engrossed me. Every characteristic listed was Michael's! They could have been writing about him. It was as if Mike Monroe had walked in and said, 'This is your life'.

With tears running down my face, I finished the booklet and lay perfectly still, staring off into space, going over and over in my mind the words I'd only just finished reading. Before too long, I knew what I had to do.

Chapter 13

Taking Control of My Life

The door to the police station was difficult to open because of the pain in my chest but I managed it. A policeman was standing at the counter writing, a pile of files to his right.

He glanced up and I saw his eyes go to the cut on my lip.

'That looks like it hurts.'

'Only when I smile,' I said. 'Lucky I don't feel like smiling.'

My statement came out in fits and starts because I was still breathing in little puffs. When I was in labour, this was how I'd breathed. Mouth open in a small 'o' puffing in and out.

'I'd like to lay charges,' I said.

He nodded and pointed to a side door then disappeared. Seconds later, the door opened and he ushered me in to a room and pulled out a seat for me.

There was a constant movement, uniformed officers moving around: behind their desks, speaking to each other loudly and casually, calling out to others entering the room with citizens under restraint. I felt inconspicuous and, until another officer sat down opposite me, almost invisible. Anonymous anyway.

Someone put a mug of tea in my hand and although I don't usually have a lot of sugar, it tasted sweet and wonderful.

I looked at my watch. Two o'clock. The boys would be home in four hours. I had no idea how I was going to explain my appearance to them, and then I brought myself up short. Why was I still covering up for that bastard? The boys knew what was going on and I was only kidding myself if I thought they didn't. Now, what hurt me more than all of the beatings was the fact that I'd put them through all this crap and they didn't deserve it. I'd put them through enough. My divorce which, for all my good intentions, had turned out to be almost as ugly as everyone had predicted. Then came a house change. Followed by this.

I leaned forward and brought my elbows down to my knees. I clasped my hands into fists and held them tightly against my mouth. I could feel tears running down my face, mixing in with my hair brushing against the sides of my face.

'Are you ready?' a soft male voice asked.

I straightened myself and using the back of my hand, smeared tears across my face. How many tears could one person produce? All I seemed to do lately was cry. I wiped again.

Some women look almost pretty when they cry. Not me. By now, my face would be blotchy and my eyes would be red and swollen. I made fists and dug my nails into my palms to try and stop from crying anymore. There is a big difference between filing charges against a stranger and filing charges against someone you had allowed into your life. But it had to be done.

Eventually the tears stopped and I could talk again. I was on a pre-ordained path and if I didn't tell my story now there might never be another opportunity. I closed my eyes and took a few breaths. Part of me wanted to blurt out everything and receive the pity I hoped would come. Another part of me wanted to run because I was ashamed that I'd allowed it to go on for so long. The fighter in me won as I remembered the feel of Michael's hands around my throat, his fists on my face, my panic and my pain. I remembered thinking how I wanted to die, remembered *wanting* to die because then there would be no more pain. There was two of me, one wanting to give up and the other determined to fight.

The next two hours went quickly as I told in detail what had happened and what had been happening for eighteen months. I told my story in a strange detached voice, aided by the prompting of the policeman as he typed.

'There,' he said at last. 'Once we hand these to him, we'll take him around to your house and wait while he gathers his things together. Any idea where he'll be right now so we can present him with these orders straight away?'

'He'll be at the shop.' I gave him the address. 'Before he did this,' I pointed to my face, 'I told him I wanted him to buy me out. Now, after you deliver these papers to him, I can't go back there at all. I just don't trust him.'

'I think that's a given.'

'When you hand them to him, would you also tell him that I won't be going back to the shop? I don't even want to talk to him.'

'I think that's very wise.'

As he stood up, he said, 'Now all you'll have to do is find yourself a solicitor. When there's a date set for the hearing, we'll contact him and he can take over from there. Any questions?'

I noticed that his eyes were intently watching me for a reaction so I nodded. I don't know if I got up unaided or how I actually managed to leave. I remember walking on leaden legs to my car, gulping to stop myself from crying again.

The next thing I remember is leaning my head against the cold window of the car and letting the tears fall.

Chapter 14

I'm Free

Within days of laying charges against Michael, I received papers in the mail from him stating that he was prepared to buy me out of the shop. That and my front door key. Apparently, a real estate agent had already valued it and a stocktake had been done. The total amount had been split evenly down the middle. All I had to do was sign the papers and return them to his solicitor for processing.

As you can imagine, I didn't stand there dithering for long. After a quick phone call to Brian Metcalf, my solicitor, I signed and posted them that afternoon, against Brian's advice. His recommendation was to send them to him for perusal and to then quibble over the price. I had no such thoughts. I wanted Michael out of my life without any delay. Now that I'd started down this path, I was anxious to sever all ties with him. Bad enough that I'd have to face him in court without compounding it with the sale of the shop as well.

This was my opportunity to crawl out of the past and make something of myself. The wolf sniffing at the door inside me. Sniffing and raising a paw. Beginning to scratch.

Visions of a holiday on the Gold Coast with the boys popped into my head. I could see myself laying on the beach under an umbrella, the boys laughing and happy as they ran in and out of the water. I could almost hear the thunderous crash of the waves on the fine grained sand, feel the fine mist beading my face and smell the mixture of seaweed and salt water.

Then sanity prevailed. There'd be no holiday. The money would be needed to pay the bills until I found a job. A job that probably wouldn't pay much because I was unskilled in anything except the hospitality trade. Even then my prospects would be diminished by the fact that I couldn't work nights. I had my boys to think about.

My next dilemma would be 'what am I going to do now?' And so, one month after I rid myself of Michael, I bought a little coffee shop, with a certain amount of uncertainty, and my days were fully occupied from five in the morning to three in the afternoon while my two boys were at school.

Some people might have enjoyed the hour of peace while doing the baking in the morning, before opening the doors at 7.00 a.m., but I was troubled by ghosts. I tried quieting them by turning up the music and singing loudly along. Even then, sometimes, the clanking chains could still be heard. Although I'd managed to cope pretty well, my ghosts appreciated these quiet times best of all. They don't like the hustle and bustle.

For this, I hated Michael most of all. Hated him for robbing me of the simple pleasure of being able to forget and let my mind wander. Just to sit quietly on the veranda and watch my boys play basketball. I found that hard to do because before long, my ghosts came out and prowled restlessly around.

Before you know it, grief ambushes the heart without warning, triggered by a scent, a sound, a memory. I never know if memory helps or hurts us. Perhaps both. In one respect you remember the helplessness and utter desolation but you also know that it is something you've overcome, even though painfully. On the other hand, you hurt because what happened was so unfair and you were stupid enough, and gullible enough, to let it go on for so long.

I've often wondered at the human capacity for stupidity. Without even knowing it, I'd created my own private Styx, the river of hate from the Greek Mythology that I'd read about in school. My soul had crossed over from the land of the living to the realms of hell.

Chapter 15

Listening Is the Best Support

As I remembered, I listened to the tink of rain-drops on the tin roof of the shop. Lightning flashed again on the horizon and the sky had turned a bilious shade of green heralding a possible shower of hail.

'What you're going through right now is despera-tion,' I said to Kelly. 'Believe me, I know. You feel like it's all your fault and it's your responsibility to fix the problem. But there's always going to be something else that's going to happen and you'll be back where you started from. The reality is that nobody can change anybody except the person themselves. You get to the stage where you're obsessed with avoiding the little things that upset him. If you know how he likes his shirts ironed, then you iron them like that. If you know he likes steak and mushrooms, then you give him the steak, and live on bread and butter if you have to, if it saves an argument. You learn how to manage the little things that you've got control over. And you *can* control it, for weeks or maybe months on end. But then things begin to happen. You may have left too much fat on the steak or it wasn't cooked exactly how he likes it. Then things get out of control and there's no way from stopping what's coming. The storm arrives and you're back where you were again, bruised and beaten and feeling like it's *your* fault the damn steak wasn't perfect.'

My voice had risen slightly and I had to force myself to calm down. But it wasn't easy. It had been damn hard to look at this young girl and not see myself in practically the same state only months before. I made excuses for Michael. I'd reprimanded myself for my negligence. I'd vowed to try harder. Why is it that women minimise the result of male violence?

I took a breath and continued more calmly. 'You start to believe it's your fault because there's no-one else telling you anything positive and because you look at your man and he's there telling you it's your fault. So eventually, you believe it. It's very hard to go against it. Most of us are raised to believe that a woman is supposed to do this, that and the other. But somewhere, it has to stop. Only yesterday, when I came home from work late, you should have seen the look on my boys' faces because their afternoon tea wasn't sitting on the table waiting for them. So I looked at them and said, "What? You can't butter some bread and put jam on it yourselves?" Sooner or later, you have to let people look after themselves a little and you have to learn to shed the blame you feel.'

'I just don't know what to do.' I could see tears

welling in her eyes but I knew pity wouldn't solve her problem.

'Wait here a minute.' I stood up and walked into the back room and dug around in my purse for the number of the policewoman I'd spoken to in the hospital. Back in my seat again, I handed the card to Kelly.

'Every situation is different, Kelly. This policewoman went through what we've both been through and she managed to help me. But her situation was different from mine and mine is different from yours. What helped me was reading a booklet outlining the full issues of domestic violence. It explained everything for me: from recognising abusive behaviour, dealing with it, preparing for emergencies when they happen, getting help afterwards and staying free.'

I could see the doubt in her eyes. She would already be thinking, 'Where will I go?' and 'How will I cope without a job?' Sometimes, this final step is too difficult to make, so the questions 'Do I stay' or 'Do I leave' are never asked.

'You have to talk to someone about this because, more often than not, it doesn't go away by itself,' I said softly. 'I really hope this is a one-off for you but all research shows that abuse is serial.'

They say support has many aspects. It can be specific like giving the name of someone who can help or it can be about helping them understand that different kinds of help are available depending on the circumstances. People often say, 'Oh my God, why does she put up with that? Why doesn't she just get out?' but when you're in that situation yourself, nothing is so black and white. If you can help them see it clearly for themselves, you help them make the connections and they begin to realise, 'I *am* in a bad situation.' So, listening and sharing someone else's experiences puts it all into its right perspective.

In a way, I think the most supportive thing that I did for Kelly that day was to give her the name of someone she could trust: someone she could talk to about her problem. Someone else with similar experiences to hers, so that she would feel that she wasn't the only person that this kind of thing happened to. And that it's *not* okay. That it's *not* how things should be.

But leaving, or going back and staying, were decisions that Kelly had to make for herself. Every woman is the principal expert in her own life and though I'm not saying that any woman in this situation should leave, I know that only the woman who has felt this abuse can know the full extent of the danger.

Kelly had already heard, 'I'll try harder' and 'It'll never happen again' and 'Everything will be okay'. And who knows, maybe it would be okay. But a lot of the time it isn't. What Kelly didn't know yet was that even if she made the decision to leave, the abuse sometimes doesn't stop there. More often than not, the abusers become stalkers, following you, entering and damaging your property, phoning you and threatening you with more physical harm. Being stalked can be a new crisis which can wear you down even further.

I knew this all too well. I knew the terror of waking one day to find your life changing yet again. Knew the possibility that judicial orders in civil and criminal courts, like the help from the police, can sometimes be useless. Knew that despite protective orders, people are sometimes violated and hurt after leaving abusive relationships. Even though these mechanisms are a strong statement that you want no contact, things can still happen.

Chapter 16

Judgement Day

Low hanging, metallic-looking clouds had turned the sky a pale grey and completely matched my sombre mood. Standing on the courthouse steps, I steadied myself against the breeze, strong enough to tug at my clothes, before I took one last breath to fortify myself and walked towards the automatic doors that concealed the court rooms. I passed through the metal detectors and entered the lobby.

The hallway outside the courts was teaming with lawyers and citizens. Everybody was on their mobiles. The tiled floor and high ceiling seemed to take their voices and multiply them until the noise surrounded me.

Brian Metcalf, the solicitor I'd hired for my divorce and now for the court case, was already waiting for me and at the other end of the room. So were Michael and his solicitor, a female no less.

I found myself wondering why he'd chosen a female lawyer. He had no respect for women and the fact that he had one representing him would have seemed funny if I'd been capable of laughing.

In the minute that it took for Brian to produce the papers, I'd sized her up. She was small with dark hair worn short and brushed behind her ears and dressed beautifully in a suit with low shoes that emphasised her tiny build. Then it occurred to me. She'd been chosen specifically to highlight the fact that this small petite *woman* trusted and believed in him enough to represent him against another woman who was charging him with assault. Tactics.

She looked calm and confident, unlike me who fidgeted with my skirt and hair. I looked into Michael's eyes and saw them narrowing, his lips tightening. He looked cool but I was shaking and cold inside.

I saw Brian look at the name above Court 1 and frown.

'What?' I could sense his unease.

'I wish we'd drawn a better judge.'

'What's wrong with him?'

'Nothing. Let me worry about it.'

Not exactly confidence-inspiring, so by the time it was my turn, my hands were icy and I'd begun to tremble. I could feel panic flowing. I looked like I was in withdrawal from either drugs or alcohol.

The years hadn't been kind to the judge but then again, I don't think he'd been a Mel Gibson to start with. His features were hangdog and his nose was bulbous. He sat imperiously eyeing me with dark sunken eyes as Brian and I sat in chairs indicated by the bailiff. Michael and his solicitor sat to the left of us across the aisle.

Brian stood up and stated my case—essentially a synopsis of the charges already filed and one the judge would have in front of him. When Brian sat down, Michael's solicitor stood up.

'Your honour, what this case comes down to is real people err. People who realise their errors and learn from them. In a moment, of excruciating pain, my client made a mistake. He has regretted this mistake ever since. And while it disturbs me to say this, the crux of the problem is that this defendant doesn't just hate my client, she would do anything and say anything to harm him. It's the defendant's bitterness and warped sense of reality that should be on trial today.'

'I object, your honour,' Brian began spluttering as he stood up. 'This is a clear case of...'

'Sit down, please, Mr Metcalf. You have had your say now let them have theirs. There'll be no objections except from me.'

I sat there listening to those incredible statements in amazement. And to my horror, Michael's solicitor went on.

'Please be aware, my client takes all responsibility for his actions and he would like to make a small statement to this court.'

'Oh, for goodness sake, Your Honour...' Brian tried again.

'Sit *down,* Mr Metcalf!' Then to Michael's solicitor, 'Please proceed.'

Michael stood up. 'I have no justifiable excuse for what I've done. I have almost gone mad with remorse. I felt duped, suicidal and double-crossed. One minute I was wanted, the next I was told to leave without any of my belongings that were in her possession.'

My mouth opened in silent protest. So much left out.

'But as I said, that is no excuse and I am so terribly sorry for what I did.'

And he looked sorry. I'd seen that same expression so many times before. I could also see the understanding expression of the judge. Even Brian glanced at me, then away quickly when he saw I'd noticed.

'She is the good one, your honour. The innocent one and I made her a victim which I regret and will have to live with for the rest of my life. I have made her suffer but I am seeking counselling to remove this cancer from my life and I ask the court's understanding and absolution for what I have done.'

Damn you Michael! We don't need your commentary, I thought. How, after that little speech, could I stand up and tell my side of the story without sounding like a vindictive bitch.

The judge cleared his throat before commencing again. He looked over at me above his glasses and asked me, 'I have read your complaint. Do you have anything else to add?'

I opened my mouth to speak but Brian answered for me. 'Nothing else, your honour.'

I glared at him. How dare he lightly dismiss me like this? There was plenty I wanted to add. How about, this attack wasn't the only one. How about, it was the last in a long line of assaults. And how about, how am I going to protect myself in the future? There was no time for me to protest because the judge began speaking.

'I don't know many men who could have stood up and said what you've said in this court today, Mr Sorensen. I would say you deserve a pat on the back not a reprimand. I think it's time to stop beating up on yourself and begin forgiving yourself for your provoked attack.'

This wasn't how it was supposed to go. I'd seen TV cop shows. I'd watched Hill Street Blues and LA Law. What happened to right being on the side of the innocent?

'Continue with the counselling and I am sure you will begin to feel the healing process. Have your counsellor send the reports to this court and I will review them on a monthly basis.'

The judge sat and looked over at me as if I was a pile of trash. A woman who was a part of the movement against the needs and wants of men. One of the women who sucker the poor men. Men, who get up early every morning, go to work, bust their guts and come home to listen to the whining and complaining of the women. There is only so much pushing and pulling a man can take. It was all there, written all over his face before he turned his attention back to the file on his desk. He didn't even look up again as he closed the file and said, 'I'll review the file in a month's time. In the meantime, Michael Sorensen,' he looked over at Michael, 'you will maintain a distance of no less than 300 metres from the plaintiff.'

I walked out of the court room, my back ramrod straight and my eyes staring in front of me. Even then I could feel the stares of every other person waiting their turn to be heard.

Once out of the court room and the front door, I rushed over to the railing, my arms folded over my chest and my heart pounding in my chest, waiting for Brian to catch up to me. I could feel tears pricking behind my eyes.

I heard footsteps approaching and I whirled around. 'What happened in there, Brian?'

I couldn't keep the anger out of my voice. I was livid. Instead of coming away with justice on my side, I'd been made to look like I'd deserved everything I'd received. 'I'm the injured party here. Why don't I feel like I've been treated fairly?'

'He out-manoeuvred us. Simple as that.' He looked down at his feet as he spoke. 'I was going to suggest counselling to the judge but as you saw, I wasn't given the chance.' He looked up at me and began to straighten his tie. 'That's it, Trisha. But be assured, he had better continue the counselling or he'll be back here again before he knows what's hit him.'

'And what do I do in the meantime? Wait for Michael to come back and finish the job he started?'

'He won't. He's been given a warning here today and if he's smart, he'll move on without looking backwards.'

'If you knew Michael, you'd know how stupid that remark is.'

And it *did* sound stupid, didn't it? Through eighteen months of hell, he'd convinced me every time he was sorry for all the abuse he'd dished out. Just as he'd convinced the court today.

Chapter 17

The Fiery Red Dot

I was feeling uneasy. This happened occasionally and although it's an unpleasant feeling, usually it's nothing I can do anything about. I'd had dinner with the boys, watched TV with them and put a Dire Straits tape in the cassette player while they had their showers and got ready for bed.

Tony, my youngest son, sat up in bed with his new Christopher Pike novel and when I said, 'Lights out in five minutes', grunted softly but lifted his head for my soft kiss on his forehead before I walked into Mark's room.

My eleven-year-old looked up at me and said, 'Do we have to listen to that music?'

'Dire Straits?'

'Whoever it is.'

If asked now if it were true, I know he would deny it, but at the time his favourite group was Bon Jovi, to be replaced (thankfully) by Eddie Vedder and Pearl Jam in later years.

'That's Mark Knopfler.'

'He stinks.'

Charming, I thought. With a smile, I replied, 'He's got

a big nose but he can really play a guitar and you'll love him when you're older.'

To that, he pulled the covers over his head and said, 'If it doesn't send me mad before then.'

Once the boys were settled, I began pacing nervously around the house.

Tiredness was beginning to take over and my attention was wandering towards the renovations I wanted to do, the impatiens budding in the garden and the new coffee shop I'd bought.

The phone rang once before I quickly picked it up, hoping the boys wouldn't wake. 'Hello?'

'How're you feeling Trish?' Michael's voice was heavy with sarcasm.

'Go to hell!' I imagined him slipping from a foothold and pin-wheeling down, face first, into an abyss. After all I'd been through with Michael, it surprised me that he could still hurt me so much and that I could bruise so easily.

'I'm simply enquiring out of concern, Trish.' I heard him chuckle. 'You looked ready to blow in court today. I don't like to see you so stressed out. Maybe *you* should see a counsellor.'

I slammed the phone down and looked outside the

kitchen window. The trouble with fear is it's everywhere, in every shadow. It wasn't only what I saw or heard that scared me. It's what I felt. A creeping sensation as if Michael was lurking in the darkness. But if he had been in the front yard, the outside light would have illuminated him. I pulled the curtains closed, feeling like a bug highlighted on a microscope slide.

It wasn't easy to put him out of my thoughts. The anger was still too fresh, and my mind continually strayed to the events of the day, but I managed. I fingered the remote control and channel surfed through Fox, finally sitting back in disgust. How can there be absolutely nothing decent on thirty-four channels? I stood up and opened the fridge surveying the contents. Nothing interested me.

Finally I went around and checked the doors for the second time that night. I thought I might as well have an early night, tucked up in bed with a book I'd been meaning to start for over a week.

I did a last check through the curtains, noticing all of the other houses were well lit, calm and peaceful, when I spotted a small red dot at the entrance to my driveway that shone brightly but then disappeared.

I squinted at a grey shape but couldn't focus on it. If it was a man, why had he stopped right there? And what was the red spot? Then suddenly it occurred to me. A cigarette! When you draw in, the end burns brightly.

I went outside and crept to the edge of the balcony and craned my head over the edge. I could hear the crickets and a far-off barking dog. There was the faint smell of some night-blooming flower, probably jasmine, in the air and the rich damp smell of earth and things growing in it. Out in front of me, over the veranda railing, there was a section of darkness and a few stars. The air was moist enough to take on a glow of its own, like that of a street light through fog, only softer, subtler, so that what little light there was at night from porches and street lights disperses and reflects off everything. It was from my balcony, in that light, that I saw a man's shadow.

In an instant, I knew it was Michael. I saw him lift his cigarette to his mouth with exaggerated care. I saw the angles of his face light up in the red fiery flare as he inhaled.

All at once I was terrified and I didn't really know what to do. Was he watching my house? Was he watching to see who came in and out or was he simply biding his time? There was something indefinably menacing about the way he just stood there.

Sick with panic, I ran into the kitchen, my breath ragged in my throat. Everything seemed in slow motion. Picking up the phone, dialling the police station number, waiting for someone to answer the ring. Everything seemed to take an age.

I looked in the mirror and a stranger with hollow wild eyes stared back at me.

'The Redlands Police Station. Can I help you?'

The male voice sounded annoyed as if I'd interrupted his favourite TV program.

'Yes. I need you to send someone out to my house right now.' I could feel myself beginning to jabber. I do that when I'm anxious. I talk and talk and I can't seem to stop. There's this voice inside my head saying 'shut up' but I can't. I just talk more and more. 'I broke up with my boyfriend a few weeks ago and now he's stalking me. He's on the footpath, just standing there. He's out there watching my house.'

I felt my chin trembling but I was determined not to cry because, to the police, it would look like weakness, what they'd call 'femaleness', instead of what it was: rage and panic. The last thing I wanted was for the police to think I was as close as I was to losing control.

I swallowed and blinked. Then swallowed again.

'Has he threatened you in any way?'

'Not tonight. But he has hit me quite often when we were seeing each other. I even pressed charges.'

'But has he threatened you tonight?'

I saw where this was going. 'That's why I'm ringing you.' I could hear the mixture of panic and anger in my own voice. 'To stop it before it gets to that.'

'He's on the footpath, you say?'

'That's right.'

'Not on your property?'

'For goodness sake! I need your help here. You're job is to protect the public and I need that help right now!'

'Ma'am.' His voice was so patronising, I felt like screaming. 'Whoever is on your footpath, and we haven't even confirmed it is your ex-boyfriend, is on public property and not even in your yard. He has made no threats to you or your property but you want me to waste taxpayer's money by sending out a patrol car to talk to someone who may very well be just walking his dog. I can't arrest someone for something you think he *might* do.'

I heard him clear his throat. 'With all due respect,

the imagination can play strange tricks on a person when they're alone.'

It sounded like something from a bad horror movie. The fact that he was patronising me made me all the more furious.

I felt a surge of intense irritation as I said, 'He's not walking his damn dog. It's *him* and he's stalking me.'

In the distance, the red dot glowed again. I could hear the policemen on the other end of the line breathing loudly as if he found this all very tiresome.

I took a deep breath. 'So what you're saying,' I began again, 'is you have to wait until he enters my property and assaults me, or worse mind you, before you can help me?'

'Sorry ma'am.'

I slammed the receiver down, my hands sweaty and my heart pounding. I sank to the floor, my legs not able to support me anymore. After sounding so together on the phone, my mind had turned to slush.

Slowly, I pulled myself to my feet. The knife drawer lay right near my hand so I opened it up and took the largest one I had out of the drawer. If he came anywhere near me tonight, he'd soon find out that he'd gone too far this time.

A drink would help, I thought. I put the knife down and dug around in my cupboard for a bottle of Merlot I knew was there and managed to uncork it without stabbing myself more than twice. The first sip was delicious, and I closed my eyes, just to savour it. It was warm with a crisp flavour, fruity and mild. The second sip made me thirsty so I gulped the rest down in one go. The next glass of wine went down smoothly but my nerves were still frazzled.

'That's what you need,' I said out loud just so that I wouldn't feel alone. 'Get completely drunk just because you're scared and then not know what the hell is going on around you.'

I recorked the bottle and put it back in the cupboard.

That night, the knife slept on a pillow next to me, my hand closed over the handle. If there was a dragon coming into my castle, I was going to slay it.

Suddenly, I was looking up at the ceiling with no memory of dreams while I slept. A sleep of the dead they call it and that's how I felt. Dead inside, drained and exhausted. Still clutched in my hand was the knife and it's a wonder I hadn't stabbed myself with it.

I forced myself into a sitting position, my body feeling as though it wasn't even mine, unwilling to get out of bed. My limbs were as weak as if I'd gone fifteen rounds in a boxing ring with Mike Tyson. And lost.

The light outside was diffused and I remember thinking it must be early. On my side table the clock read 4.20 a.m. I'd had all of four hours sleep. No wonder I felt disorientated.

I decided to have a shower to try and wake myself up. I fiddled with the knobs trying to get the temperature right, veering between boiling hot and freezing cold. Eventually, I got it right and closed my eyes and leant back against the tiled wall while the shower pummelled on my shoulders leaving me feeling human again while I savoured the warmth. I've always loved showers. The sound soothes me, like a downpour in the rainforest.

Finally, I forced myself to turn off the taps and I reached out to pull a towel from the towel rack. Condensation had covered the mirror and my eyes became riveted to what I saw.

HELLO

The words had been written on the mirror. Terror clutched my heart and I quickly wrapped the towel around me as if hiding myself from a camera in a corner.

Michael had written the words, I knew. I knew! But when? While he lived here? Or could I have slept through his movements in the night? It would mean he'd had a copy made of the key he'd handed back to me. Damn it! Now I'd have to change the locks.

I felt as if I was in a bad movie, standing shaking in a puddle of water pooling around my feet as I stared at the words, imagining Michael walking around my house in the dark hours of the night. Looking at my boys peacefully asleep in their beds. Watching me while I slept fitfully, clutching the knife. How had I not heard him?

My first instinct was to check on my boys. Still with the towel around my body, I ran from the room, slipping and sliding in my haste to get to my children.

Through the thumping in my chest and the ringing in my ears, I watched them both sleep quietly. No sign of anxiety on their faces, just the sleep of the innocent except for the fact that my youngest had started sleeping with a baseball bat on the floor beside his bed. Toys were scattered around their rooms. They were both hanging onto the Ninja Turtle stage. They had Donatello sheets. Raphael curtains and the action figures were always visible somewhere.

If I'd paid more attention to my boy's habits, I would have seen things a little more clearly in the beginning. Even when I hadn't heard Michael's car, I could tell when he had arrived. I could tell the way some people can tell if it's going to rain. Like a dog who knows when his master is home, only reverse that. Instead of running to the door in anticipation, my boys did the opposite. They got out of the room fast. Even if they were watching a TV program they liked, they ran. You see, I thought I knew better.

My next instinct was to call the police again. But even as I moved towards the phone in the kitchen, I knew it would be useless. They'd made it clear enough last night that they wouldn't come out to my house unless a definite threat had been made and even though those words were still evident on my mirror, there was no real threat in them. And how could I prove he was the one who'd written the words? Even *when* he'd written them?

I walked back into the bathroom and angrily wiped the words away. The squeak my hand made felt like a cleansing and my reflection stared back at me.

Dark shadows had formed under my eyes and even to myself, I looked ten years older than I had six months ago. Michael had once said that I had an Olivia Newton-John look about me but if he could see me now, he would have denied ever saying it.

'He will never hurt you again,' I said to myself in the mirror. I watched my lips form the words, watched each muscle in my face change as my mouth moved.

I finished dressing, feeling less than human but knowing I had to keep going, make the lunches for the boys and head off to work. When I looked at the clock, I was surprised to see it was 5.00 a.m., only forty minutes after I'd woken up.

After scribbling a quick note to the boys, I locked the front door and walked down the steps towards my car. It was then I noticed the flat tyre.

I wonder how long it's possible to live in a world where nothing makes sense. There's a philosophy that says everything is pre-ordained. Fate, some people call it. My personal philosophy is that it's easy to believe this when things are going great. It's easy to look around when you're happy and say there's a meaning to everything, 'meant to be' even. But when your life is a nightmare and you can't see any way out, all that goes out the window. For instance, look at Biaffra, Auschwitz, and Chernobyl. Are they a part of God's great plan?

The church says, 'God moves in mysterious ways'. But why *does* he? Why *should* he? Is there a reason for torturing innocent people? Hard-working, well-meaning people?

I sighed and returned to the kitchen, turned on the kettle and called RACQ to come out and change the tyre. I'd never changed a tyre in my life, wouldn't know where to start.

With a fresh cup of tea in my hands, I walked back downstairs and waited for them to arrive.

The clouds looked like undulating sheets of tin in the sky. Just before the sun broke over the horizon, the wind suddenly died and the sky became as pale as bleached bone as if the colour had been drained out of it.

I stood in the yard looking at the trees towards the front of the property, where I'd seen the tiny pin-point of Michael's cigarette the night before. The tree trunks were a few yards back from the footpath and the morning sun was low on the horizon, sneaking under the foliage and veiled with mist. Standing on the driveway, I moved aside a branch of the Leopard tree and stared down at the dark soil and the sparse alyssum that was scratching out a life in almost constant shade.

Then, through the dappled shade and the unraked leaves, I saw shoeprints less than a yard away. They startled me, my heart thumping good and hard as I looked. They were side by side, facing the steps, like someone had rested there and waited, or an invisible man was standing there right now, offering his hand to shake. Or raising it in anger to strike me. Men's footprints. Big and fresh. Proof that Michael *had* been here last night, to me at least, but it wouldn't be enough for the police. The prints could have been made by anyone, they'd say: a salesman, a neighbour. Anyone. Even if they spoke to Michael, he'd smile that winning smile of his and laugh with them. He'd tell them to read the court transcripts, read what the judge had said. After that, they would have no time for me and my suspicions, no matter how real they were.

The sound of tyres crunching on the driveway brought me back to the present. The RACQ had arrived. One hour later and behind in my schedule for the day, I drove my Nissan Pulsar up Mount Cotton Road in the coolness of the morning, the gum trees silent and still in the morning light as if painted against the sky.

The weather wasn't going to improve, so the radio announcer said. I can take any defect in a car but it has to have a radio. I needed sounds and voices, especially today. I needed noise to fill the void, to stop me from thinking too much. As I moved through the traffic, I tapped my fingers on the steering wheel in time with Madonna singing 'You'll see'. Kind of appropriate, I thought at the time.

For a while, trying not to think of where my life was headed seemed hard. I can distract myself with TV or work but eventually thoughts and memories creep in as they did now. My wolf, sniffing at the door yet again. As I drove, the wolf breathed over my shoulder, panting. Today a wolf, tomorrow something under the bed or in a closet, lurking under the dark surface of a cup of coffee.

As I parked my car behind the shop and got out, my wolf jumped out and disappeared.

The morning progressed as normal and during a lull, I placed a sign on the door that said 'Back in 5 minutes', took the tyre out of the boot of my car and rolled it into Lenny's Car Repairs around the corner to have the puncture repaired.

'You look stressed.' Lenny, grey-haired and in his mid-fifties, was an absolute darling. I didn't need to know that I looked a mess, especially since I had to greet customers all day long looking like this.

'Pretty much as I feel today.' Automatically, one of my hands strayed to tidy my hair. 'Can you repair this some time today? If I don't get it done today, I just know that I'll have a puncture on the way home and then there won't be a spare. The way things are going, I'd take bets on that happening.'

'Sure,' he smiled. 'Just come and get it before you go home. It'll be ready.'

The day dragged on endlessly, the hands of the clock limping their way around the face. I'd downed enough caffeine to stay awake for a week and still I felt exhausted, although jumpy, when my morning regulars came in.

At eleven o'clock Billy arrived. Everyday, Billy walked up and down the counter looking at the contents of the hotbox, silver whiskers festooning his jaw and making whistling sounds through his pursed lips, until he finally pointed to the roast and said, 'I'll give that a try.' Everyday, his routine, and his lunch, was always the same. Without fail or variation.

Then Victor came in. Three generations ago, Victor's family emigrated from Scotland but Victor, now aged sixty, still wears a tartan vest proudly. Everyday, he sat with Billy for over an hour drinking endless cups of tea and talking.

Then Barry, the station master, came in with a new blonde joke.

'Hey Trish, why do blondes go through so much shampoo?'

I placed my hands on my hips and said, 'Okay, Barry. Why do we use so much shampoo?'

'Because the instructions say, "Wash, rinse, repeat." Get it?'

I put on my usual look of mock indignation which pleased him no end before he waved and moved on to some other unsuspecting blonde.

Even Harvey came in. Harvey was a nice enough guy, close to eighty and lived a short walk from the restaurant. Twice a week, he spent most of his day at my shop, reading the newspaper, shaking his head and trying to engage people in a conversation over anything from the price of petrol to terrorism. Today, he sat in his spot turning the pages of the paper and shaking his head as usual.

'What would you like today, Harvey?'

'Just a steak sandwich,' he said. 'White toast.'

'All the trimmings?'

'No beetroot. I'll only wear it,' he said looking down at his white shirt.

'Drink?'

'Coffee later.'

I nearly made it back to the kitchen.

'Trish,' he called out. 'Come over here.' He was pointing to the chair opposite him so I reluctantly turned and walked back over. Billy was smirking at me as he wiped his own plate clean. 'What can I do for you, Harvey?'

'Look at this,' Harvey said poking a finger at an article in a newspaper folded awkwardly in front of him. 'Another plane crash in the States.'

'Do you know I've heard that it's statistically safer to fly in a plane than it is to drive your car?' I informed him.

He shook his head at my density.

'Point is, the papers are telling us anything can happen these days. Just like that murder down in Sydney. Anybody can go to bed at night and wake up and there's a dead body waiting for you.'

I nodded. I had no wish to engage in a conversation

going in *that* direction and I was saved from answering when another customer came in. I stood up and said, 'I'll get your lunch, Harvey.'

Five minutes later, I placed his sandwich in front of him and he continued the conversation as if I'd never left. 'People think they can change things but they can't. They make things bigger, faster or keep you alive longer. But even then, you can still wake up with a dead person.'

'You're a philosopher, Harvey,' I said as he took a bite of the sandwich.

'Used to be an accountant,' he answered scanning the paper for more disasters.

I looked out of the window and Crazy Clark's looked back at me. In my mind's eye I could see myself walking from the train station with the dozens of other young girls on a day-outing from the orphanage. Once a month, Sister Philomena marched us to Woolworths, each with a shilling in our pockets. Once a month, we lined up at the train station to go back to the convent and eat the sweets we'd bought while we sat in St Bernard's Hall waiting for the monthly movie to start. That was when I was ten.

It seemed lots of old ghosts were bothering me today. I remembered the squalid flat where I grew up until

I was seven. I remembered the many foster homes I'd lived in until the age of fifteen. Even in my teens I was considered a little uncouth. Not that that worried me. I've been called worse things than *that* in my life.

'Look at this. Look at this,' Harvey said, finding more truth in the paper and pulling me out of my reverie. He spoke with the quiet certainty that he knew everything vindicated his philosophy.

I picked up his empty plate and napkin.

He glanced up and said, 'Watch out for yourself. Won't make a difference but it can't hurt.'

'You've brightened my day, Harvey,' I smiled.

'You're welcome,' he replied.

The clock said it was a quarter to two. That only left me time for a quick sandwich before starting to clean up if I was going to be out of the shop by three o'clock to pick up my tyre at Lenny's.

Chapter 18

The Enemy Awakens

The shop had a only cursory clean that day because I wanted to go home to my boys. But first, I had to go to Lenny's to pick up the tyre, then a last minute stop at the shops to collect some items that I needed the next day and then I could head home and relax. A glass of wine, dinner with boys and a long hot shower before an early night. Who said I was hard to please?

I walked into Lenny's shop. 'Hi, Lenny. All done?' I tried to sound chirpier than I felt but even to my own ears, the tiredness still came through.

'All done,' he said. 'You got an enemy?'

I could feel my heart plunge then catch on something, feeling as though it dangled lopsided by a single thread. 'What do you mean?' I croaked.

'This tyre of yours. That was no puncture.'

'But it was. It was as flat as a tack.'

'It was flat all right.' As he was talking, he walked over to a tyre leaning up against a wall and rolled it over to me. He picked up a screwdriver as he continued talking.

'See this?' He pointed to a hole in the old tyre and pushed the screwdriver easily through. 'That hole wasn't done by anything as small as a nail. If you ask me, someone deliberately wrecked your tyre and he, or she, used a screwdriver to do it.'

I closed my eyes and rubbed my forehead. I had to try and think straight. Again, going to the police was useless. I had absolutely no proof that Michael had done this, but in my heart I knew. He'd watched my house last night, walked around inside and put a screwdriver through my tyre before he left. What would he do next?

'Oh God, Lenny. When is it going to end?'

That afternoon, every street I passed, every corner I took, every stop sign, I expected to see him standing there, smiling his smug smile at me. I found myself scanning my rear vision, as I reached the vicinity of my home. I found myself caught between *hoping* I'd see him so I could contact my solicitor to add to the growing list of my complaints and *scared* that I'd see him and know for sure he was stalking me.

When I got home, I walked into a nightmare.

Chapter 19

He Returns

I told myself I wasn't seeing what I thought I was seeing as I stepped over smashed crockery, broken glass and pools of milk, juice and water in my kitchen. Everything I could see had been screwed up, stamped on or damaged beyond repair.

This can't be, I told myself again as I looked around in wide-eyed disbelief. I'd spent weeks speculating and re-speculating, my fears rising as the days passed, whether Michael was still capable of hurting me, now that he was no longer in my life. I'd played over in my mind and rehearsed scenarios where I met him somewhere, anywhere, and I was prepared for whatever dangers he might throw at me. I had started blithely to believe that nothing bad could happen to me now. It hadn't occurred to me that he was capable of this sort of senseless damage.

As I stood in the kitchen, alert for any sound or movement in the house, I was uncomfortably aware that this could be the start of a new plan of attack from Michael. My surroundings seemed to recede and I felt like I was being lifted up to the ceiling and I was staring down at myself. The only thing that kept me halfway sane was the thought *Is he out there right now, lurking in the late afternoon shadows, watching and laughing at my terror?* My eyes jerked to the window, imagining movement in every shadow.

Worse still, would he come back tonight to finish what he'd started while I sat in scared silence waiting for his approach? Darkness is the most effective disguise.

I took a deep breath to slow the ones that were coming too fast. Even though I was close to the brink of hysteria, I felt a surge of anger surpassing all of my other emotions. My boys stood behind me and, as I turned to hold them back with an outstretched arm, their looks of astonishment and uncertainty moved me into action.

Suddenly, my mind was sharp and clear, free of the emotional detritus of the past few weeks. I remember the sound and feel of glass and crockery cracking beneath my feet as I walked over to the phone to call the police.

Unlike yesterday (was it only yesterday?) when the indifferent reception I'd received from the police had sent me to the sanctuary of my bedroom with the knife in my hand, today's assault had motivated me to be positive and proactive. Even though I was still frightened, I had come to realise that I couldn't, and wouldn't, give in. There was nowhere to hide. If I cowered, I would be nothing but prey.

'The Redlands Police Station. Can I help you?'

Yes. Give me energy. Give me answers. Give me peace, I wanted to scream. Instead I said, 'Yes, I'd like you to send someone out to my house. My house has been broken into.'

I looked back at the boys, still motionless at the front door. Trying to move them into action, I waved my hand at them in the direction of their bedrooms and mouthed 'Check out your rooms' as the voice over the phone said, 'What's the address?'

I told him, stopping short of mentioning the phone call from last night. The last thing I needed was to get his back up before they'd even arrived.

Half-an-hour and a hundred angry circuits of the loungeroom later, two policemen stood at my door surveying the damage. 'Have you had a look around to see if anything is missing?' one asked.

'This isn't a normal break and entry. My ex-boyfriend did this.' I waved my arms around to show them the extent of the damage done. Cups, plates and glasses had been taken out of the cupboards and smashed, the entire contents of the fridge was all over the floor and, in my bedroom, the remains of the clothes Michael had bought for me in his attempt to change me into what he wanted me to be were shredded with a pair of scissors that had been left on top of the pile of clothes.

They both observed me politely. The one who was doing all the talking so far asked, 'How can you be so sure?'

'Look for yourself,' I said with more assurance than I felt. 'All of my things have either been smashed or ripped. The only things missing are *his* record albums and the bits and pieces that belonged to *him*.'

The two policemen exchanged a glance.

'He broke in and did this to my home and I want him arrested!'

'We're going to have a problem with that,' the talkative one said.

'What do you mean a problem? He did it. So charge him.' I wanted to shout and scream but instead, I breathed deeply in and out.

'That may well be correct but without evidence, there's not a lot we can do. For a start, he didn't break in. He used his key…'

'It was *not* his key,' I interrupted. 'He gave *his* key back to me. Apparently, he had another one cut before he did so.'

'So be it. What I'm trying to say is he didn't break in. He used a key. Secondly, he took nothing that didn't belong to him, just his personal things.'

'But what about the damage?' I was angry and frustrated and I wanted to snap at him for being so condescending.

'Not enough to charge him, I'm afraid. If we go to him with this, all he has to say is he was with some friends at the time, who will no doubt back him up, and then you've got nothing.' His face was deadpan. 'Have you spoken to the neighbours? Did anyone see him at all?'

'There aren't any neighbours on one side, just a vacant lot. The other ones both work during the day,' I snapped.

The reality of my situation was setting in. Michael would escape from justice again. He'd escaped from the assault charges and now he would escape from this.

'All I can suggest is to change the locks as soon as possible so he can't get in again,' the talkative one continued.

Did he shrug or had I imagined it? I wasn't sure what astounded me more: his cavalier response or his lack of concern for my plight. In my present frame of mind, it was like throwing petrol onto an open flame. If this were a movie, the director would have had Will Robinson's robot in the background waving his arms and yelling, 'Warning, Will Robinson. Warning.'

'And what is to stop him from coming back again and again if he thinks he's left something else behind?' I asked angrily. 'Is he allowed to just walk in here whenever he wants to because he thinks he's left a cigarette lighter behind? Or a biro? Or even some item of clothing? When will it all end and where is the safety I need for myself and my children?'

When he spoke, it was with a tired drawl as if the words were almost too much trouble to utter. 'We'll talk to him ma'am but that's all we can do. As I said, have the locks changed and the next time it *will* be a break and entry.'

For the second time that day, I found myself trying to compose myself.

Next time? Next time!! I was flushed with rage at what I saw as the police fobbing me off. I would like to say that I was contemptuous but I was becoming too panicked at the thought of 'Next time' to carry it off. I could feel the anger coming and I was afraid I wouldn't be able to stop it. Plus, I didn't want to. It wasn't sharp and clean like they say in books. It wasn't cleansing. It was heavy and cumbersome as a wagon full of rocks. Like once I was pointed in that direction and let go, I'd never get back. What I needed to do was point my anger at someone. At the policemen who stood so nonchalantly in front of me. At Miles for even damn-well introducing me to Michael. At Michael for coercing me into making the worst judgement of my life. At myself for being foolish enough to believe the lies he'd fed to me.

I could feel the saliva drying up in my mouth, more solid than liquid, and knew that this time my voice would emerge as a falsetto.

So I was silent as I watched them leave.

Chapter 20

The Fight Back

Nature's least likely fighter is the rabbit. This animal is made for defence with its camouflaging coat, ears that rotate to hone in on any threatening sounds, and eyes that see for 360 degrees. It's even a herbivore with chiselling teeth and claws that are intended to claw at leafy pants. But when it's cornered, where there's no chance of flight, it will attack its adversary with a shocking ferocity. Physical abusers are the worst kind of adversary and I was going to show Michael just what he was up against. There comes a time in your life when you know that you have to stand up and be counted.

At some point, I told myself I'd had enough. Consider a person without a sense of limit. Isn't that what it is to be a monster? Someone whose anger and pleasures have no restriction, no boundaries?

I had reached my own limit. The way I saw it, awful things had happened to me and these awful things needed to be stopped. That was my moral voice speaking, my super-ego. Was I going to let him get the better of me once more? *I don't think so, Tim,* I thought; that oh-so-trite, smart-ass reply.

After shooing the boys back into their rooms, I picked up the phone and called Brian.

'Brian? I want you to write a letter to Michael's

solicitor for me,' I began after his receptionist put my call through to him.

'What sort of a letter?' I could hear the uncertainty in his voice but that wasn't going to stop me. *I* was in charge now.

'Michael was in my house last night while we were all asleep and punctured my car tyre before he left. He must have had a key cut from the one he gave back to me. Then, this afternoon, after I'd picked up the boys from school, we got home to find that he'd been in the house and smashed whatever he could get his hands on.'

'I want you to call the police,' he said unnecessarily.

'I've already done that. They were no help whatsoever. Apparently, he only took what was his and they wouldn't be able to prove it was him who broke in.'

As I spoke, there was an emptiness in my heart like a cold grey dawn. No more would he put me through this pain. No longer would he be able to control my life.

'The letter I want you to write is to state what happened here last night and today and to inform her that it has been reported to the police. I want you to say that the locks have been changed and that any future invasion will result in charges of breaking and entering being laid against her client.' I was starting to feel the buzz of progress. 'I want you to send it out to her tonight so that she gets it in tomorrow's post. Say it however you want to, only make sure the point gets across. He is *never* going to do this again, Brian.'

'Don't worry. I'll do it straight away. See if you can get a locksmith out this afternoon to change the locks. But I honestly feel that this was done to shake you up and he's succeeded. He has no need to come back tonight. It would be more advantageous for him to leave you wondering when the next attack will be. I'll call you when I hear anything.'

After I hung up, I felt stronger. More in control of my life. More like myself again. Be damned if I was going to be a pushover any longer.

Thanks to Michael, it was close to midnight by the time I'd finally cleaned up and crawled into bed. It seemed like an eternity since I'd risen at 5.00 a.m. this morning but, on the upside, tomorrow was Friday and then I would have two days off.

Chapter 21

His Last Attempt

The boys both had basketball games on Saturday, so I dropped them off while I went down to the Redlands Park to do some shopping. I returned half-an-hour later, rosy-cheeked and sweating under a cloudless humid sky and stopped to retrieve any mail from my letter box.

I opened the flap and leant down to glance in. I never put my hand in anymore ever since a large hairy huntsman greeted me one day by running up my arm and disappearing inside my cleavage. This time, however, it wasn't a spider I saw. Inches from my nose, a huge rat, gazed back at me, its eyes glassy and its fur patchy with blood, but most decidedly dead. A white piece of paper arranged on top of the body in a perfect upside-down V said, 'This could be you too'.

I staggered backwards, a scream working its way up from my throat and I landed on my butt. I must have staggered back to the car but I don't remember doing it. Minutes later, I was down at the Police Station talking to the same policeman I'd seen only a day ago.

I refreshed his memory about what had happened, starting with the phone calls and the late night visit, the punctured tyre and finished with the damage to my house he'd seen only too well with his own eyes.

He breathed noisily through his nose as if he found this all very tiresome while I told him about the rat in my letterbox.

'What do you want us to do?'

'What do I...' What sort of stupid question was that? 'Well, I'd have thought you would come back to the house and take the note and do whatever it is you people do with evidence. It's *his* writing and it's blatant harassment. I want something done this time. How many times does he have to do things like this before you people help me?'

He listened without expression, then said, 'Okay, okay' in a bored voice. 'We'll send one of "our people" down with you to check it out. Just a moment please.'

I threw my head back and squared my shoulders righteously. 'Thank you, officer.'

He seemed to be gone a long while during which time my mind raced without getting anywhere. I was just about to go back to the counter and ring the buzzer again when another policeman came through the door and asked with a condescending smile on his face, 'Are you the lady who reported the dead body, ma'am?'

I tensed briefly, then said as tersely as I could, 'My

car is out front. You can follow me.' I turned abruptly and walked away listening to the sound of his shoes behind me, clicking in time to mine.

I parked my car on the grass, allowing him to park in the driveway in full view of the letterbox. I watched him unfold himself from the police car and walk over, squatting on his haunches while he opened the lid and peered in.

As he stood up and walked towards me, I wound my window down but said nothing. He put his hand on the roof of my car and leaned down.

'This is where the body was, you say?'

That wasn't what I'd expected him to say. 'Well...yes.' I stammered. 'Why?'

He smiled laconically but, because of his dark sunglasses, I couldn't see his eyes. 'I've done a thorough search of the building,' he said, smirking more as he continued, 'and I've found nothing... Ma'am.'

'But... but that's impossible. It *was* there before I went down to the station. I saw it clearly.'

He turned away and made a remark, his voice too low for me to hear, then turned back with a grin on his face. 'With all due respect ma'am, there's no body there now.'

The fact that he was trying to patronise me only made me furious.

'I know what I saw,' I snapped. 'I want to see for myself.'

He stepped backwards as I jumped out of the car, pushing him aside in the process, and stormed over to the letterbox.

I stood looking down at the empty letterbox. 'I know what I saw. I didn't imagine it,' I said lamely.

'Well, maybe so, but there's nothing we can do about it. I suggest you take your groceries upstairs and make yourself a cup of tea.'

I was angry and mystified and I wanted to snap at him but I bit my lip because to be honest, he was right. What *could* I do?

'He must have come back while I was at the station and taken it away.'

'I'll tell you what. If anything else turns up, phone us and we'll come down.'

'Whatever,' I said as I wafted my hand in front of my

face. I hated hearing his tone of forced tolerance. 'Thanks,' I said a little belatedly.

The wind was picking up and on the horizon, dark clouds were gathering so I quickly took the groceries upstairs. Surprisingly, I drove steadily and calmly to pick up the boys. However, as soon as I cut the engine in the parking area, I found myself trying to compose myself as my body shook violently. How long would it be before Michael realised I was out of his life forever? How long before he stopped scaring and degrading me?

After a series of deep breaths, I braced myself and walked inside the stadium to the sound of hundreds of boys bouncing their basketballs all at the same time.

Any mother with two energetic boys between the ages of eight and eleven will know what I mean when I say I woke on Sunday morning to a grey, dismal rainy day, knowing I was going to have my hands full keeping the boys occupied and away from each other's throats.

By ten o'clock in the morning, my house looked like a Toys'R'Us store had exploded into my livingroom. By eleven o'clock, the sounds of shrieks and thumping feet filled my ears and I knew I had to do something, and fast.

I mouthed the 'bad word' and another choice curse from Michael's repertoire and walked into Mark's room to police the noise. They were both red-faced, their fists flailing as they kicked each other on the floor. At the sound of my raised voice, they separated as if they were spring-loaded.

'Mum, Mark hit me,' Tony howled.

'He hit me first,' Mark pointed at Tony and yelled.

'What did I tell you both about fighting? What's the matter with the two of you? Can't you spend one day together without trying to kill each other?'

'But it wasn't my fault! You always take his side, just because he's the youngest,' Mark wailed.

'He threw my biscuit out of the window,' Tony cried a little louder.

'That's because he was writing his name on my window with it,' Mark jumped in.

'Enough!' I yelled at them both, my hands up in the air palms outwards as if I could hold back the onslaught. 'You're driving me insane. Get out of this room. Now.'

There were toys everywhere and I had to shuffle some of them out of the way to make a path through the action toys, small metal cars, picture books, Lego and Castle Grayskull so they could leave without touching each other and start round two.

'Another magic Sunday,' I mumbled as they passed me on their way through. When they behaved like this, they slipped into a category called 'not for general viewing'. All I could think was that even at my age, no doctor in his right mind would knock me back on a tubal ligation.

I picked up a half-eaten peanut-butter sandwich as I walked out of the bedroom door.

There's nothing like junk food to calm the savage beasts, so for lunch we had hot chips with gooey toasted cheese sandwiches, a culinary delight the boys loved, then we all curled up in front of the TV with a pile of videos, cheezels and coke—wine for me. This combination, I confess, was the highlight of my weekend.

Monday morning came and I let the front door of the coffee shop rest gently against the door-jamb behind me as I walked in. I always left the door not quite closed so that the Cobbitty Farm man could deliver the bread and rolls as he always did, first thing every morning.

But it wasn't the bread man who walked in five minutes later.

From the kitchen, I heard the squeak of the front door opening and called out, 'Three loaves of white, two wholemeal, one multigrain and two dozen rolls, thanks John.'

There was no answer but seconds later, Michael stood in the doorway of my kitchen.

He walked over to me, grabbed my wrist with one hand and, with the other, wrenched off the delicate gold bracelet that he'd given to me for my birthday last year.

'If you don't want anything more to do with me then you won't want this, will you?'

His face was a livid red and veins were popping out on his forehead. If he'd dropped to the floor right now of a heart attack, I wouldn't have done a thing to help him. Months ago, I would have been terrified by the sight of him and, to tell the truth, my heart *was* hammering hard inside my chest. But my new-found resolve had taken over and, deep down, I knew that he wouldn't go too far in my shop. I hoped anyway. You see, by now I knew he was a coward and he had crossed a boundary that he shouldn't have. All he could do now was to try and scare me to save what little dignity he thought he had left.

He stood in front of me, panting, while I tried to control my own breathing. As I stared back at him, I was determined to rid myself of the fear he'd instilled in me over the past eighteen months.

'I want you to know that I will be contacting my solicitor about your visit here this morning,' I said with a hell of a lot more confidence than I felt. 'You have broken the court's decree that you are to remain more than 300 metres away from me. Apparently, you think you're above the law.'

The tic in his eye was distracting me but it meant that I was getting to him.

Unfazed, I continued. 'I am going to instruct my solicitor to write yet *another* official letter to yours and state that this is your final warning. If you come near me, my shop, my house or my children again, I will have you back in court so fast you're head will spin.' I wanted him to know that my finger was on the pulse and the toe of my shoe was up his butt.

I pushed past him, hating the feel of his body warmth as my arm brushed his chest, smelling the nicotine ingrained in his skin and the raw odour of perspiration that seemed pressed into his clothes.

I expected him to grab my hair as I passed, and was amazed when he didn't. I walked on jelly legs around the counter to the front door, holding it wide open, as much to support myself as a safety move to allow any passers-by to hear and see everything.

'I want you to leave. Now, Michael. Right now.'

As he stepped closer, I smelt a stale odour in his clothes as if he'd slept in them, that is, if he'd slept at all. But I stood my ground.

'You do, do you?' he sneered, a look of amused malice on his face. I closed my eyes to blot out the image.

'I want you to leave right now,' I repeated.

'I haven't finished with you yet.'

So damn sure of himself.

'I WANT YOU TO LEAVE NOW!' I yelled. My head was high, as noble as my patrician namesake, and I stared at him blatantly; straight in the eyes. A hound on the heels of a wounded fox. All bluff, of course, but entirely convincing because incredibly, he stepped back from me as he glared. But this time it was different. He was less convincing in his act of condescension. More defeated than threatening. Only subtly, mind you.

I stood there trying to hide my shaking hands, staring steadily at him as he stared back at me with his hands balled into fists. I could see his pulse beating in his throat but I tried to keep my eyes flat and my expression empty, while inside my chest, my heart bounced against all of my ribs.

Then, he actually blinked. As long as I live, I will never forget that look. It will forever be my inner comfort. He knew his control over me was over. He knew there would never be another time when I would cower under his physical strength or wince at the cruel words he might throw at me.

Without another word, he walked out of the door leaving me to slam it shut and push the bolt home.

Chapter 22

Kelly's Choice

The storm that had been threatening for most of the afternoon arrived with full tropical force. Rainwater rushed through the drainpipes, flooding the gutters and pouring down unrelentingly. The wind howled as if in unison with the emotions that Kelly had been feeling inside the warmth of my shop. People huddled under the veranda outside, their clothes hugging their bodies tightly, while they waited for the downpour to abate.

'I have to go.' Kelly stood up abruptly as she glanced at a clock on the wall. 'I've been here too long.'

'But it's raining. You'll get drenched.' I was stating the obvious, I know, but I don't think Kelly was even aware of the storm raging outside. She was already on her way to the front door.

It was as if I could read her mind. She was in her 'clean-up' stage: coping with what happened. Denying and minimising it to herself but not yet to the 'do I stay or do I leave' stage.

'I can't stay any longer. Jason will be wondering where I am and then it'll start all over again.'

Even as she spoke these words, the realisation of what she'd just said stopped her in her tracks. It made her hesitate for just a second before turning back to me.

'That's what you've been trying to tell me, isn't it? That it could start all over again.'

'I hope it doesn't, Kelly. I truly do. But you can't pretend it didn't happen.'

She held up the card I'd given her and stared at it. 'This policewoman will be able to find that booklet for me, you say?' Her eyes were moist as they looked up and searched mine.

'I'm sure of it, Kelly.'

She nodded slowly before saying, 'Thanks for listening to me. I *will* ring her.'

At that, she turned back to the door and disappeared out into the rain.

Epilogue

Nowadays, I find myself thinking of my life and what I've made of it. In the first year after Michael's departure, I would call up his face when I felt lost and hopeless. Whenever I sat, I'd let my mind wander. I would soon think of him. Even when I hated it. Even when I tried to make my life go forward, the memories tugged at me. Then, I reminded myself of how low I'd been and I used his memory as a prod to rise above my misery. How lucky I was to have survived *that*. To feel depressed, I reminded myself, was pure good grace.

My life has changed and I've changed with it. Grief about other things has replaced my grief for what Michael did to me and has reshaped my thinking about how life should be lived. Now and then it comes back to me and, as I conjure up Michael's face, I realise that we should never let go that which has shaped us, we shouldn't forget those experiences. We should only learn from them.

People who are not directly involved may believe that domestic violence is not the serious social problem that it is. They might think this violence is either a predominantly lower-class phenomenon, caused by alcohol, or is something confined to other ethnic groups, some more so than others. This is certainly not the truth although there is a lack of accurate statistics due to the hidden nature of the problem. Even so, it is clear that domestic violence can, and does, happen to women in *all* social classes and between one in three and one in ten families are affected by it. People perhaps assume, wrongly, that this problem is for working-class people only, because these are the women most likely to seek help from agencies. But it *does* happen to middle-class women: they are just less likely to ask for that help because of the shame and embarrassment it causes and because of the possible damage to their husband's careers if it's disclosed.

Another myth is that battered women have done something to deserve the beating, may even have provoked the man. But a survey done in the mid-1980s shows that one in every three domestic incidents was not preceded by an argument. Even so, violence is not an acceptable method of resolving a conflict and nobody asks for, or deserves, abuse.

Economic dependence is by far the main reason a lot of women stay. Some women are justifiably scared that leaving will not end the abuse. They find themselves in a 'Catch 22' situation where they are abused if they stay but then followed and terrorised if they leave. Statistics show that nearly half of all women murdered by their spouses are, at the time, separated or in the process of separating.

All too often, a woman knows she will be pursued by the enraged man, aided and abetted by his financial superiority and his friends. She has to uproot herself and, quite often, her children; all with varying degrees of shame, low self-worth and low self-esteem. When asked why she didn't do it before, her reply will nearly always be, 'because I thought it was my fault'.

So, considering all of this, the real question we should be asking is, how on earth do any women manage to leave at all? But why do we never ask that question? Why do we always throw our hands up in horror and disbelief when someone we care about keeps going back for more? I believe the hiding, the shame we feel, the covering up and denial of abuse are themselves often the biggest obstacles to breaking that control and, because of these factors, the myths of domestic violence have arisen.

What a lot of people don't realise is that these violent men can appear totally remorseful after an attack. But this regret and remorse does not result in real change nor does it mean he will abandon the control that he has in the relationship. The woman is then confused by his show of love and sensitivity and will willingly stay in order to feel that warmth her partner awards her, even though she knows it doesn't mean he is going to change permanently. They prefer to ignore the violence and hope that, by doing so, it will go away. But even with the best therapeutic help, change is usually slow and difficult.

Unfortunately, domestic violence is not new. It has existed for centuries and this dreadful problem has been hidden and ignored because the victims have deliberately chosen not to bring the crime out into the open. Role-modelling has a large part in this. Examples of behaviour in the form of attitudes, interests, goals and prejudices have been handed down to us by our parents. Boys are supposed to be 'masculine' and are expected to be sporty and independent. Girls should be 'feminine' and are often taught to be passive and less aggressive. Men make the decisions and women follow. Even organised religion has condoned the belief, based on the teachings of the holy books, that the physical chastisement of women is acceptable. But what can be learned, can be unlearned.

Although my booklet said there are Seven Steps to Freedom, I believe there is one more. The final step, the eighth one, should be, 'Making a new life for yourself and learning to trust again'.

How many times, after something you regret doing,

do you say, 'I'm never doing *that* again'? Some women choose to remain alone rather than take the risk of another potentially violent relationship. The funny thing is we're not meant to be alone. We all crave human contact and denying ourselves that pleasure is another way of letting the abuser win yet again.

Eventually, we have to learn to trust and move on; get our heads together. Think, Maybe one day I'll meet someone else. Begin to look at other men and, instead of thinking, Will he hit me?, start thinking, He's rather nice.

Part of me *is* still the person who was a victim of abuse because it's something hard to forget, but I just don't *feel* like that person anymore. I see things differently now and I see myself and the world differently. Sometimes I look back at the person I was and I feel sorry for her. Sorry that she could have such low self-esteem that she could let someone treat her like that. At one level, you feel wonder that you could spiral down into such helplessness but at another level you realise that you have to let the memories help strengthen a resolve that it will never happen again.

Now, when these memories come back, I don't let them drag me down. I recognise them as shadows of something I've freed myself from. I use them as a re-inforcement that I'm a survivor and that I've come this far and will never go back.

The most important thing of all is the learning process in recognising the shit when it starts flying about. As hard as it is, you have to understand that you're in a mess. You have to make the decision to wash yourself down, clean yourself off and get yourself out of it. Accept the fact you may wear the smell for a while and learn to recognise that smell again. You have to have commitment and direction. What happens too often is people take themselves out of bad situations and put themselves back into the same situation again. Just like the alcoholic we see lying in the street. But this doesn't have to make you feel like a drink; it can also make you more committed to *not* have another drink. Use that first whiff of something foul as reinforcement of your desire to succeed, *not* as something that drags you down.

Thank God, that period of my life is well behind me now. I've come through the bad part and managed to rebuild my life. I've come through the storm and found peace again. I'm now happily married and know first-hand that love can come again.

The Seven Steps to Freedom

Step 1: Identifying abusive behaviour

First, because some forms of abuse are subtle, they can easily be denied and, at first, many people do not recognise it for what it is. They may only know that they don't like the way their partner treats them. Aggression, anger, intimidation, manipulation and control are the main patterns of abusive behaviour leading victims to feel afraid and dependent on their abuser.

Abusers do not necessarily seem domineering or aggressive. They can be attractive and charming. They can be businessmen, doctors, lawyers, policemen, mechanics or labourers. They may be a blind date, a neighbour, or worse still, a family member. Abuse can occur among people of any culture, profession, or religion and is not restricted by age, class or social standing. It can happen occasionally or repeatedly; every month, every week or every day.

Contrary to some popular opinion, abuse is a learned behaviour. It is an attempt to establish domination and control over its victim. This mistreatment can break down a victim's sense of self-worth and self-confidence. Victims, however, avoid coming to terms with the abuse because there is usually an attentive stage filled with regrets and promises: reasons to deny the abuse is happening.

But during this stage, the pressure is rising. Tension increases in this build-up stage and victims tend to stay out of the way to prevent an attack, but the truth is that there is no escape. The abuser will explode at the peak of this cycle using words or physical violence.

Then there is the calm or 'honeymoon' stage when denial, embarrassment and regret sets in. Abusers may show kindness, offer apologies and promises of no further abuse thus confusing the victim but, above all, leading the victim into a false sense of new hope in the relationship. They often even blame the victim for initiating the abuse as well as denying and minimising the damage.

The next part is the clean-up when coping is back in place. But old habits and patterns soon resurface. Life may go on as it did before but another explosion is imminent and the next incident may be worse than the last.

Step 2: Recognising abusers

Surveys have been done and the results show that the majority of abusers are men; in fact, women are ten times more likely to be victims than men. Abusers often grew up in violent families and were abused as children. Violence is a learned trait but it can be treated.

Abusers may use different types of abuse.

First, there's physical abuse that takes various forms including hitting, pulling hair, slapping, breaking bones, burning, twisting arms, throwing victims against walls and throwing objects or weapons. It also includes destroying property and denying human needs such as nutrition or medical help. For many, there is the constant threat of death or serious injury because of the seriousness of the attack.

Another form of abuse is verbal consisting of insults, constant put-downs or derogatory remarks about the victim's lack of attractiveness, incompetence or inability to cope on her own. This constant humiliation can destroy a woman's belief in herself until she eventually believes that she is worthless and that it is all her fault.

Psychological abuse cannot be ignored and is closely related to verbal abuse. It leaves the victim with no self-confidence or self-esteem and with the belief that she is stupid or useless. This abuse accumulates over a lengthy period of time and the damaging consequences are longer lasting than the physical ones.

Then there is social abuse where verbal abuse occurs in front of other people in the form of jokes and put-downs or criticisms about the woman's weight, intelligence or appearance. The abuser controls the woman's life by isolating her from her friends and family; often she cuts herself off for fear of angering her partner. Some men go to the extreme of regulating visitors to the house and monitoring phone calls thus controlling the flow of contact and lessening the victim's ability to leave. Even when or if the victim does manage to leave the relationship, the abuse often continues in the form of damage by words, hands and weapons, maintaining their control by retaliating against the victims for leaving them.

Abusers share common characteristics. Initially they may appear kind, affectionate, sensitive, and thoughtful, showing social charm and winning personalities but frequently they exhibit different behaviours that show selfishness or a lack of empathy towards others. They have a low level of tolerance for the mistakes of others and are quick to anger over trivial matters. Perfection is expected, leading them to set impossible standards. Their behaviour is inconsistent keeping their victims unsure and afraid to make any decisions in case this leads to another bout of violence. Their good traits and sometimes kind behaviour often lead victims to minimise and deny their abusive ways. Abusers may appear protective and concerned for the welfare of their victims by taking charge of difficult situations but, ultimately, leaving them unable to make independent decisions of their own. This subversive behaviour controls their victims because, instead of honest communications, abusers resort to manipulation. However, they take no blame for what happens afterwards. They make others responsible for mistakes and anything that goes wrong. Abusers often blame circumstances, life and even their victims for their own reaction to stress.

Their intensity of emotions and lack of emotional self-control are danger signals that should be noted. They are silent volcanoes ready to erupt at any time.

Another trait is jealousy and wanting excessive time with their victims involving no-one else, which leads to obsessive or possessive behaviour. They attempt to keep their victims from friends and family. They lie habitually and avoid conversations that may expose their past.

These common traits are the warning signals that should be heeded.

Step Three: Preparing for emergencies

People respond to violent crises in different ways. Some run, some hide, some fight back but events sometimes take an unexpected turn so you may be unable to behave as you had planned. You may be overcome with fear, unable to move. You may be unable to call for help or gather your children and belongings or even grab your car keys. An attempt to leave may save your life or it may put you in more danger but if you make it through a violent crisis, you often become stronger and wiser: a survivor.

An *emergency plan* is a short-term one. It covers you and your children during the violence. A *safety plan* is more long-term but both plans should be prepared in advance. They can be worked out alone or with the help of professionals familiar with domestic violence.

It wise to remember that safety plans don't guarantee your safety because abusers may become violent without warning. When arguments begin to escalate, you should remain near safe exits. Think ahead and practice what you will do in the event of an attack.

Part of a safety plan is having a network of help available if you need it. Your safety plan should also include backup ideas if shelters are full or motels are unavailable. Set aside some money for food and petrol and other expenses and keep your plan to yourself or include only those whom you can count on in an emergency.

Step Four: Getting help after a crisis

Physical violence can inflict damage that is not immediately recognisable but may be potentially lethal. Such medical conditions are often difficult to determine because of shock and trauma. During abusive incidents, your body may release levels of natural chemicals that act as painkillers. These reduce pain and camouflage the seriousness of the injuries so it is important to seek professional medical and dental treatment, both to assess damage and obtain documentation for possible legal processes. You should not bathe or shower, but instead keep any torn or bloody clothing and seek medical advice. From there, emergency or temporary housing, day-care for children, money and employment could be sought.

Social service agencies and church groups can help provide assistance with food, clothing, etc. Shelters, hotlines and advocacy groups are available to help and can usually be found in the white pages under Social Services. They provide counsellors and offer sanctuary that may evolve into comprehensive programs of assistance.

At this point sometimes doubts begin to set in and many women return to their abusers. Questions like How will I survive financially?, How do I protect myself and my children from future attacks if I leave?, Where will I go? and Will I be believed?' filter in and in a lot of cases that final step is too difficult and terrifying, so they return to the devil they know rather than the devil they don't.

What victims need to know is they can eventually lead healthy and happy lives after they go through a healing process and they *will* become stronger because of it. They look back on their abuse with the realisation that it is over although some victims leave and return to their abusers many times before finally becoming abuse-free. It requires work and commitment if victims and batterers decide to stay together. With education and support, there is a possibility that abuse can stop and the relationship can resume but this is not done without intervention and treatment.

Step Five: Making the decision to stay or leave

'Do I stay or do I leave?' That is the question asked by most women. Making changes and taking action is not easy. People who are abused often love and hate their abusers at the same time. Anger, confusion, fear and hurt all create a turmoil of emotions that never stabilises into any semblance of order or logical result.

For most women, leaving their home can be a

complex decision influenced by financial and custodial concerns and it is important to think clearly. It may be beneficial for the victim to stay in her home and remove the abuser but usually it is safer to leave the home, although abusers often escalate their destructive behaviour with this option. The first concern should always be the safety of the victim and her children.

For these reasons and also because they have many years invested in the relationship, victims often decide to stay with their abusers. They want the abuse to stop but the relationship to continue. Most hope that the kind side of their abuser's personality will prevail and the battering will stop. They fear the far-reaching strength of their abusers and worry that they will face continued or escalated abuse if they leave their relationship and that their children will suffer in the process. They fear that they do not have the ability to survive financially especially if they do not have a career or an earning capacity and there is a lack of support from their family who believes that they should stay and work things out.

Many women who have experienced childhood abuse are more willing to accept abuse as an adult. Their boundaries and beliefs about what is acceptable may not be as clearly defined as those who grew up in non-abusive homes. They are psychologically fragile so they doubt their own abilities. They believe there is no help available and create a lonely existence for themselves leaving them vulnerable to danger, further abuse and long-term brainwashing.

Contributing to their confusion is the batterer's behaviour which is often contradictory, shifting between kindness and abuse, a Jekyll-and-Hyde personality. They confuse compassion, loyalty, love and duty with their own need for emotional and physical safety believing that by being patient and loving, they can help their abuser.

Overly kind and compassionate people may be targeted by manipulators and batterers. They don't want to believe that someone they love would harm them and will not change. Such denials are common in victims and are supported by embarrassment and shame. Ultimately they take the responsibility for their abuse. This is reinforced by comments from the abuser such as 'If you hadn't done that, I wouldn't have hit you' or 'It's your fault because you're so clumsy'. Victims begin to think things like 'If only I'd kept my mouth shut' or 'If only I'd kept the house cleaner' and immediately assume responsibility for the abusive treatment. In the end, they often decide to stay and try again instead of facing the alternative—leaving their abuser and starting a new life.

Assessing relationships takes learning to sort out the complex feelings and emotions such as fear, anger, disappointment, sadness, hope, loss and insecurity. You may be showered with gifts and promised many things in the future and love, hate, and fear your abuser at the same time. Thinking clearly in the midst of confusion and chaos is not easy and should be done with professional help if possible.

Few people accept loss willingly and there is often not enough recognition about the extent of the loss. Victims may lose trust, innocence, and belief not only in a person but also in the very existence of love. They lose homes, friends, years of accumulated possessions, the ability to pursue their own goals, feelings of identity, their health and their self-esteem.

All of these emotions are contributing factors in decisions about whether to stay or go but it is important to put these losses into perspective. If you stay in an abusive relationship, you also lose a great deal.

Step Six: Learning to heal and rebuild

There are stages of grief after escaping from abusive relationships. Denial is usually the first stage, as is a refusal to accept what is happening.

Anger follows denial. Victims may be angry at another person, society, themselves, their parents or the situation and this anger can be misplaced or inappropriate.

Bargaining often follows anger and is an attempt to negotiate or change the outcome and severity of loss.

Depression is often the next and more lasting stage and can become a physiological condition. It can feel overwhelming that someone you loved and trusted could violate you and is unwilling to change. This depression can be devastating and can have physical symptoms such as chest tightness, hysteria, weight loss and mood changes; you may cry excessively or experience lethargy and a change in sleeping habits, even exhaustion. Professional help should be sought if symptoms of depression continue or interfere with daily functioning.

Acceptance is the completion of the grieving process when a person acknowledges the pain and hurt of loss but has adjusted to the change in circumstances and can face the future. You realise that mistakes can be made and are a natural part of the healing and rebuilding process. You may have developed learned helplessness after having been put down or told you were wrong so often that you find it difficult to maintain a healthy sense of self-worth but evaluation and self-knowledge are powerful strategies in healing. Remind yourself that everyone makes mistakes and find ways to learn from them; be kind and patient with yourself. Read books, build support systems and focus on finding purpose in life. Make a list of inexpensive activities that you enjoy, eat and sleep well, exercise regularly and relax.

Leaving a batterer will not ensure your safety so additional caution can save your life. Victims who choose to separate from their abusers and remain in their homes should develop home safety plans in case the abuser returns to inflict further harm. It is vital not to minimise the level of your abuse and danger.

Being stalked can present an ongoing crisis and can wear victims down and turn them into vulnerable prey. It can come in the form of unwanted following, vandalising of property, entering of property, home surveillance, unwanted contact by mail or telephone with the intention of harassment or with the threat of physical harm. You should contact the police, reinforce your home locks, document the specific times and locations of stalking, tape-record telephone calls and, if possible, not travel alone.

There are several options available in seeking help

from law enforcement agencies. Violence can be addressed in civil or criminal courts. Criminal courts can prosecute abusers for assault and battery and can provide orders for no contact between attacker and victim. A hearing is held with both abuser and victim present to make individual testimony for or against the protective order but despite having protective orders, people are sometimes hurt or even killed after leaving abusive relationships.

It is important to use all available assistance and resources during this dangerous time. Protective orders are a strong statement of a victim's determination to end abuse but contact or court orders can be ignored. Other plans should be put into place which may involve installing new locks and alarm systems, leaving lights on, developing a code that lets someone know you are in danger, getting a dog who barks and asking police to drive by often. Victims may already have been subject to terrorist tactics in their own homes and be afraid to speak their minds. It is important that this does not continue.

Step Seven: Remaining abuse-free

Remaining free from abuse may include taking precautionary measures and can mean being more diligent, less trusting and more cautious. It can mean being aware of the red flags that signal abuse in friendships and other relationships.

Guidelines include being careful about letting people know you live alone, not readily giving out your name and address, getting an unlisted phone number and asking for caller ID, being wary of people who call offering prizes or money and always locking your doors and windows. Meet new dates in public places, bring your own car or transportation and never invite a new romantic interest to your house until you are sure it is safe. Talk to a new date at length on the telephone and listen for danger or warning signals. Take your time with people, dates and friends you are becoming close to. Note how they interact with people and what other people they include in their lives. Give trust as it is earned and develop and maintain a good support system among friends and peers as well as maintaining independence and your own individual interests. Above all keep active and avoid becoming isolated.

Survivors of domestic violence can help to rebuild their lives by caring for their own emotional and physical health.

HELP, SUPPORT AND REFERRAL

Australia

NATIONAL

Police —000
Ambulance —000
Translating and Interpreting Service—131 340
Lifeline—131 114

A.C.T.

Domestic Violence Crisis Service—(06) 248 7800

NEW SOUTH WALES

Benevolent Society of NSW Centre for Women's
Health (Macarthur Area)
Domestic Violence Advocacy Service—1800 810 784
Domestic Violence Line—1800 656 463
Dympna House—1800 654 119
Kingsford Legal Centre—008 047 727
(24hr Help Line)
Women's Health Information and Resources: Crisis
Line—(02) 9699 6288
Women's Refuge Referral and Resource Centre—
(02) 9518 8379

NORTHERN TERRITORY

Alice Springs Domestic Violence Service—
(08) 8952 1391
Alice Springs Women's Shelter—(08) 8952 6075

Darwin Crisis Line—1800 019 116
Ruby Gaea House—(08) 8945 0155
Domestic Violence Service (08) 8945 6200

QUEENSLAND

Dolores House Women's Shelter—(07) 4061 1308
Domestic Violence Contact—1800 811 811
Domestic Violence Resource Centre—
(07) 3217 2544
Women's Health Centre—1800 017 676
Zig Zag—(07) 3843 1823
Domestic Violence Advocacy Service—
(07) 3217 2544
Women's Health Queensland—(07) 3839 9962
Logan Women's Health Centre—(07) 3808 9233
Relationships Australia Logan—(07) 3808 9235
Lifeline 13 1114
Murrigunyah Aboriginal & Torres Strait Islander
Women's Corp—(07) 3290 4254
Immigrant Women's Support Services—
(07) 3846 3490
Youth and Family Services—(07) 3808 9235

SOUTH AUSTRALIA

Domestic Violence Help Line—1800 800 098
Domestic Violence Outreach Service—
(08) 8267 4830
Women's Health Line—1800 182 098
Domestic Violence Crisis Service (08) 8223 2200

TASMANIA

Domestic Violence Crisis Service—(03) 6233 2529
Hobart Women's Health Centre—(03) 6231 3212

VICTORIA

Domestic Violence and Incest Resource Centre—
(03) 9387 9155
Victorian Women's Domestic Violence Crisis
Service—1800 015 188 (24hrs)
Women's Health Victoria—1800 133 321
Women's Refuge Referral Service—(03) 9329 8433
(24hrs)
Women's Resource Information and Support Centre
(Ballarat)—(03) 53 333 666
Women's Shelters: East Gippsland—(051) 52 6152
Action Centre (Melbourne)—(03) 9654 4766

WESTERN AUSTRALIA

Crisis Care Unit—1800 199 008
Women's Refuge Multicultural Centre—
(08) 9325 7716
Women's Health Care House—(08) 9227 8122
Women's Information Service—(08) 9264 1900

New Zealand

North Shore Women's Centre—(09) 444 4618

OTHER TITLES FROM SPINIFEX PRESS

Help! I'm Living with a ~~Man~~ Boy
Betty McLellan

With a mixture of sensitivity and humour McLellan puts forward some thoughtful strategies to help men understand the difference between mumbled promises of future help and solid action.

– *The Sunday Times*

ISBN 1-875559-79-5

Beyond Psychoppression
Betty McLellan

This book is a guide to therapy that explores the intersection between the personal and the political. Recommended for courses in the humanities and social sciences.

ISBN 1-875559-33-7

Long Life: Positive HIV Stories
Jonathan Morgan, Bambanani Women's Group
and Others

Long Life tells the stories of thirteen remarkable
women from the township Khayelitsha in Cape
Town who are all HIV positive. These women, all
part of the Memory Box Project, relate their stories
through the use of body maps which tell their life
histories.

ISBN 1-876756-42-X

Painting Myself In
Nina Mariette

Expressing oneself through creativity can be an
immensely challenging and satisfying experience.
Nina Mariette, a survivor of childhood abuse, uses
painting to make sense of her past, and tells a story
with pictures and words. She writes, "When I paint,
I can move to a space of freedom that I've never
felt before."

ISBN 1-875559-73-6

Shiatsu Therapy for Pregnancy
Bronwyn Whitlocke

This book is an instructive manual for pregnant women, partners and birthing partners caring for pregnant women. It is useful during pregnancy, during labour and in the months following birth.

ISBN 1-875559-81-7

Chinese Medicine for Women
Bronwyn Whitlocke

… a comprehensive guide … for women seeking an alternative to Western treatments.

– The Republican

ISBN 1-875559-70-1

Women's Circus: Leaping off the Edge
Adrienne Liebmann, Jen Jordan, Deb Lewis,
Louise Radcliffe-Brown, Patricia Sykes and
Jean Taylor (Eds.)

This is a big, rowdy, colorful, three-ring circus of a
book, packed with death-defying feats and acts
that will thrill and amaze—not the least of which is
their breathtaking commitment to feminist process.

Carolyn Gage

ISBN 1-875559-55-8

The C-Word: A Story of Cancer
Jean Taylor

I highly recommend *C- Word* as a book that ought
to grace the bookshelf of every lesbian household.

– Ruth Wykes, *Women Out West*

ISBN 1-875559-99-X

Kick the Tin
Doris Kartinyeri

When Doris Kartinyeri was a month old, her mother died, and Doris was removed from the hospital and placed in Colebrook Home. A moving testimony from one of the Stolen Generation.

With a Foreword by Lowitja O'Donoghue, Doris Kartinyeri's story allows the reader to understand how it felt to be separated from family and from the Ngarrindjeri culture into which she had been born.

ISBN 1875559-95-7

Voices of the Survivors
Patricia Easteal

Based on a national survey about rape and sexual abuse, Patricia Easteal includes the words of women who have experienced abuse from husbands, estranged husbands, relatives, dates, bosses, priests, acquaintances and strangers.
They are powerful stories from these survivors.

ISBN 1-875559-24-8

Patient No More: The Politics of Breast Cancer
Sharon Batt

The international best-selling book on breast cancer.
> Peter Thomson, ABC Radio National

ISBN 1-875559-39-6
(Available from Spinifex in Australia and New Zealand only)

The Will to Violence: The Politics of Personal Behaviour
Susanne Kappeler

Sexual violence, racial violence, the hatred of foreigners: how should we understand these and other forms of violent human behaviour?

A brilliant and original analysis.

ISBN 1-875559-46-9 (pb) 1-875559-45-0 (hb)
(Available from Spinifex in Australia and New Zealand only)